P9-EDK-095

FOUNDATIONS OF MODERN ECONOMICS SERIES

Otto Eckstein, *Editor*

NEW VOLUMES

Prices and Markets, *Robert Dorfman*
Labor Economics, *John T. Dunlop*
Evolution of Modern Economics, *Richard T. Gill*
Economic Systems, *Gregory Grossman*

SECOND EDITIONS

American Industry: Structure, Conduct, Performance, *Richard Caves*
Money and Credit: Impact and Control, *James S. Duesenberry*
Public Finance, *Otto Eckstein*
Economic Development: Past and Present, *Richard T. Gill*
International Economics, *Peter B. Kenen*
National Income Analysis, *Charles L. Schultze*
Student Guide, *Hartman-Gustafson*

FIRST EDITION

The Price System, *Robert Dorfman*

FOUNDATIONS OF MODERN ECONOMICS SERIES

RICHARD T. GILL   *Harvard University*

Economic Development: Past and Present

SECOND EDITION

PRENTICE-HALL, INC.   *Englewood Cliffs, New Jersey*

PRENTICE-HALL FOUNDATIONS
OF MODERN ECONOMICS SERIES

Otto Eckstein, *Editor*

Current printing (last digit):
10   9   8   7   6   5   4   3

PRENTICE-HALL INTERNATIONAL INC., *London*
PRENTICE-HALL OF AUSTRALIA, PTY., LTD., *Sydney*
PRENTICE-HALL OF CANADA, LTD., *Toronto*
PRENTICE-HALL OF INDIA PVT. LTD., *New Delhi*
PRENTICE-HALL OF JAPAN, INC., *Tokyo*

C

Economics has grown so rapidly in recent years, it has increased so much in scope and depth, and the new dominance of the empirical approach has so transformed its character, that no one book can do it justice today. To fill this need, the Foundations of Modern Economics Series was conceived. The Series, brief books written by leading specialists, reflects the structure, content, and key scientific and policy issues of each field. Used in combination, the Series provides the material for the basic one-year college course. The analytical core of economics is presented in *Prices and Markets* and *National Income Analysis,* which are basic to the various fields of application. *Prices and Markets,* a new book prepared especially for this edition of the Series, takes the beginning student through the elements of that subject step-by-step. *The Price System* is a more sophisticated alternative carried over from the first edition. Two books in the Series, *The Evolution of Modern Economics* and *Economic Development: Past and Present,* can be read without prerequisite and can serve as an introduction to the subject.

The Foundations approach enables an instructor to devise his own course curriculum rather than to follow the format of the traditional textbook. Once analytical principles have been mastered, many sequences of topics can be arranged and specific areas can be explored at length. An instructor not interested in a complete survey course can omit some books and concentrate on a detailed study of a few fields. One-semester courses stressing either macro-

or micro-economics can be readily devised. The instructors guide to the Series indicates the variety of ways the books in the Series can be used.

This Series is an experiment in teaching. The positive response to the first edition has encouraged us to continue, and to develop and improve, the approach. The thoughtful reactions of many teachers who have used the books in the past have been of immense help in preparing the second edition —in improving the integration of the Series, in smoothing some rough spots in exposition, and in suggesting additional topics for coverage.

The books do not offer settled conclusions. They introduce the central problems of each field and indicate how economic analysis enables the reader to think more intelligently about them, to make him a more thoughtful citizen, and to encourage him to pursue the subject further.

Otto Eckstein, *Editor*

Contents

INTRODUCTION   1

One   GENERAL FACTORS
       IN ECONOMIC DEVELOPMENT   3

Population Growth. Natural Resources. Capital Accumula-
tion.   Specialization, Division of Labor, Large-scale Produc-
tion.   Technological Progress.   Weighting Factors and the
"Residual."   Summary.

Two   APPROACHES
       TO THE THEORY OF DEVELOPMENT   23

The "Stages" of Economic Growth.   The "Classical" Theory.
Labor Surplus Theories.   Needed: A General Framework.   Ob-
stacles to Growth.   Self-sustaining Growth.   Getting Started:
Industrial Revolution, Take-off, Big Push.   Summary.

Three BEGINNINGS OF GROWTH IN
THE ECONOMICALLY ADVANCED COUNTRIES   40

*Getting Started in the Past. The English Industrial Revolution.
Beginnings of Modern Development in Other Countries. Summary.*

Four THE GROWTH OF THE AMERICAN ECONOMY   59

*The Favorable Background of American Growth.   Major
Trends in American Economic Development.   How to Account
for This Growth Record.   The "Residual" in American Growth.
The Future: Self-sustained Growth Forever? Summary.*

Five THE PROBLEMS
OF THE UNDERDEVELOPED COUNTRIES   80

*Meaning of Economic Underdevelopment.   How Poor Is Poor?
The Demand for Development.   The Obstacles to Development.   The Scale of Possible Development.   Three Key Issues.
Summary.*

Six ALTERNATIVE APPROACHES—
INDIA AND CHINA   100

*Similarity of the Basic Problems.   Contrasting Methods.
Raising the Rate of Investment.   Agriculture vs. Industry.
Population Policy. Achievements and Costs. An Important
Moral.*

SELECTED READINGS   116

INDEX   118

For most of the world's history, the central economic problem of mankind has been that of survival. There have, of course, always been certain privileged classes or individuals— emperors, pharaohs, lords, and princes—who have lived in comfort and even great splendor. There have also been periods of general economic advance when improvements in the arts and technology have brought some measure of relief to the lower orders of society. But improvement has been slow, reverses common; the Golden Age has been followed by the Dark Age; the feast by the famine. For the mass of mankind, long hours of toil and a meager return have been the basic facts of economic life.

In the modern world, however, an essentially new phenomenon has occurred. Beginning in Europe and spreading to the United States, Australasia, and a few other areas, there has taken place within the past two hundred years a marked acceleration in the rate of economic progress. In the countries affected, national production began to increase not slowly and sporadically but rapidly and persistently. The speed of expansion was so great that even though these countries were experiencing the most rapid rates of population growth they had ever known, the levels of per-capita living standards increased by leaps and bounds. The kind of advance which might formerly have taken centuries or even millennia to accomplish was now being achieved in a matter of decades. Moreover, the benefits were accruing not just to the aristocracy but to all classes of society. For the first time in history, the

1

common man in many nations was not one but several degrees removed from the level of subsistence.

It is this phenomenon of rapid and persistent economic growth which is central to the field of economic development. What are the factors which make for economic expansion? How do we account for the exceptionally vigorous progress recorded by certain countries during the past century or two? Equally important, why is it that during this same period certain other countries have shown not growth but stagnation or even decay?

These questions are far from academic. In recent years there has been an intense upsurge of interest in the problems of economic development in every corner of the globe. In the United States, in Western Europe, in the Soviet Union, in China, in the underdeveloped countries of Asia, Africa, and Latin America, the interest in economic growth is intense. In the poorer countries of the world, this is especially true. Despite their great efforts during the 1950's and 1960's, many of these countries still have not found the key to the kind of rapid development that has brought such benefits to the West. They are keenly aware of the problem and are demanding economic progress at almost any cost. The attempt to initiate large-scale development in the underdeveloped countries of the world may well represent the most significant social and economic task of the next half century.

In the following pages, we shall try to suggest some of the main points which economics has to make about the process of growth and development. The field is a very broad one, covering questions in history, sociology, and political science as well as those in economics; moreover, there is a great deal in it still to be explored. Nevertheless, the intensive investigations of the last 15 years or so have brought forth a number of interesting insights which form a necessary starting-point for any serious student of social affairs. It is this basic groundwork that we shall try to set out in the pages that follow.

General Factors

in Economic Development

The meaning and implications of rapid economic growth have become increasingly clear in the modern world. A century and a half ago the economically advanced countries of Europe and North America produced, on a per-capita basis, perhaps two or three times as much output as the less-favored regions of Asia, Africa, and Latin America. Now the gap is ten, fifteen, or even twenty times. In one area of the world, a vastly productive urban, industrial, and technologically oriented society has emerged. In the other, the ageless primitive ways of the peasant often still endure. Rapid modern development has created the "affluent society" in the West and, in the same sweep, has brought about an enormous and increasing gap between the living standards of the rich nations and the poor.

This diverse pattern of development was, of course, the product of a number of historical, cultural, and other circumstances peculiar to the various countries involved. Underlying these special circumstances, however, were certain forces which economists have found to be central to the growth process in general.

These underlying forces have to do with the size, organization, and character of a country's basic productive apparatus. Production in all societies has certain common characteristics. It requires, first of all, the existence of the basic productive agents, or *factors of production,* as they are commonly called. There must be labor, natural resources, and certain tools, implements, and

3

other capital goods. It also requires that these factors of production be organized into some kind of producing units and that there be a minimum of technological knowledge to direct the society's productive efforts. Without any one of these elements a country's productive capacity would either vanish or sink to the level of the jungle.

By the same token, economic growth can be thought of as the process of expansion or improvement of these basic productive elements. A society's output may grow because of an increase in its supply of factors of production—labor, natural resources, capital goods—or because of improvements in the organization or basic technology of production. If these changes occur rapidly enough so that there is a substantial and persistent increase in output per capita, we have the phenomenon of modern development.

Such considerations lead to a listing of certain major factors which will affect the supplies of the factors of production or their mode of utilization in any and all societies. This list would include:

1. Population growth
2. Natural resources
3. Accumulation of capital
4. Increases in the scale or specialization of production
5. Technological progress

Since we will be referring to these factors frequently in the pages to follow, we will devote this first chapter to making a few summary comments about each.

POPULATION GROWTH

It is natural to start with the subject of population growth not only because human beings serve as both ends and means in all economic activities but also because of the dramatic changes which have taken place in the world's population in modern times. It has been estimated that it took the world from the beginning of Christian times to the middle of the seventeenth century A.D. to double its numbers; at our present pace, we will accomplish this same feat in less than 40 years. In 1965 the world's population was between 3 and 3.5 billion people and its net rate of increase was roughly 1.8 per cent per year. If this pace continues, there will be, in 600 years, only 1 square yard of the world's land surface available per person. The phrase "standing room only" has begun to take on a new and rather ominous connotation.

The relationship of population growth to economic development is interesting and complex. An increasing population means, of course, an increasing supply of the basic factor of production—labor. Over the long course of history, until fairly modern times, population growth has been the major

Table 1-1 THE ACCELERATING INCREASE
OF THE WORLD'S POPULATION

Period	Percentage Rate of Increase of World's Population Over 50-Year Periods
1650-1700 ⎫ 1700-1750 ⎭	16.8
1750-1800	24.4
1800-1850	29.2
1850-1900	37.3
1900-1950	53.9

At present rates of increase it is estimated that the world's population would double (increase by 100%) in less than 40 years. Thus the acceleration of the last 300 years is still continuing today.

Source: L. Dudley Stamp, *Our Developing World* (London: Faber and Faber, 1960), p. 19.

source of such general expansions of output as the world has enjoyed. And this was because labor, assisted by a minimum of tools and working in essentially traditional ways, was unquestionably mankind's greatest productive asset. When we think of the phenomenon of modern growth, with its characteristic rise in output *per capita,* however, the matter becomes much less clear. A growing population almost invariably leads to an increasing total output, but it also makes for a greater number of persons among whom this output must be divided. It raises not only the numerator but the denominator as well. There are more productive hands but there are also more mouths to feed.

Whether the net effect of population growth on a society's level of output per capita will be positive, neutral, or even negative will thus depend on the particular pattern of the population increase and on the context in which it occurs. If, for example, population growth is associated with high fertility and an increasing number of children relative to adults, then the number of consumers will be growing more rapidly than the number of producers, the dependency burden on the active workers of the society will be heavier, and the effect may be negative. But if there is a rise in life-expectancy which extends the productive years of the workers of the society, then the problem of an increased burden of dependency may be at least partially offset.

Quite apart from the pattern of population growth are important questions about the environment in which this growth occurs. An increasing population, within a limited geographical area, can place heavy pressure on the available natural resources of a community. Also, if the society has only a small stock of tools and other capital goods, labor may have to be substituted for more effective tool-using methods of production. All this, however, may be counterbalanced by the fact that the growing population represents an expanding *market* for the goods which the society is producing. An expanding market may stimulate the society to high levels of investment in

5

capital goods which will spur business activity and increase employment opportunities and jobs. Furthermore, it may provide an outlet for the products of efficient large-scale, mass-production industries. Under certain circumstances, these effects may be more than strong enough to offset the pressure on resources or on the stock of capital goods.

We will be developing many of these particular points as we go along; the general point we are making here is that population growth may be either favorable or *un*favorable to economic development, depending on where, when, and how it takes place. In the eighteenth and nineteenth centuries, when there were vast areas of the world to be settled, population growth may often have been an important positive factor in stimulating development. In the United States, even as recently as the 1930's, economists were fearful that the apparent slowing down of our rate of population growth at that time might be a factor making for long-run stagnation. By contrast, in present-day India there is an almost universal consensus that a slowing down of population increase would contribute substantially to the country's development prospects. What might still be good medicine for some of the sparsely settled regions of Latin America and Africa might be disastrous for Japan, China, and Asia generally. In each case, one has to weigh the effects of an increasing labor supply and expanding markets against the quite different effects of pressure on resources and capital, and, of course, the spreading of any given total output over a greater number of people.

This comment, of course, has to do with the effect of population growth on economic development. But, in fact, we are on a two-way street. Economic development may also have important effects on population growth. Is there any general statement we can make in this connection?

This second question is, if anything, even more complex than the first; the issues it raises are by no means fully settled among economists and demographers. There are, however, two important points—one emphasizing the dependence of population growth on economic development, the other its independence—which are well worth having in mind from the outset.

The first point has to do with the economically advanced nations of the world and their accelerated population growth over the modern era. During the past century or two, much of the population increase in these developing countries must be attributed to a persistent fall in the death-rate, which was closely related to the economic progress these countries were making. Economic development brought higher standards of living, better food, more adequate clothing and shelter, protection from the natural disasters of drought and famine. Accompanying economic development during this period were great advances in sanitation, public health, and medical science. The combination of improved economic conditions and an increasingly scientific approach to medicine meant healthier people, longer life-expectancies, and a

6   sharp decline in infant mortality.

In general, therefore, we can say that the modern increase in population in the developing countries of Europe and North America occurred along with and was really part and parcel of a more general process of rising living standards, industrialization, and technological progress.[1]

The second point has to do with the "population explosion" in the underdeveloped countries of the present day. These countries have shown very little economic growth, yet their populations are expanding rapidly. How is this possible?

The answer, essentially, is that these countries have been able to "import" certain by-products of development from the economically advanced countries but not the growth process itself. More specifically, the spread of Western techniques of public health, sanitation, and medicine to the underdeveloped countries has brought sharply falling death-rates and rapid population growth *even in the absence of rising living standards and the other accompaniments of economic progress.* As it is sometimes put, these countries are having a "public health revolution" prior to and independently of an "industrial revolution."

Some examples: In Ceylon, over the past 30-odd years, death-rates have declined from roughly 30 per 1,000 of the population per year to 10 per 1,000. Ceylon's anti-malaria campaign, involving a comparatively simple use of DDT, lowered the death-rate in the malarious parts of the country by 11 per 1,000 in a period of only 5 or 6 years. In Taiwan, from 1906-1910 to 1941-1943, death-rates declined from 33.4 per 1,000 to 18.5 per 1,000. In the 20 years from 1940 to 1960, Mexico's death-rate dropped from 23.2 per 1,000 to 11.4, Costa Rica's from 17.3 to 8.6, Malaya's from 20.1 to 9.5, Singapore's from 20.9 to 6.3. All these declines are of a very high order of magnitude but they have not in any way been correlated with the rate of economic progress these countries have been making.

This point is of great importance. Although the modern acceleration of population growth has its ultimate roots in the general economic and technological expansion of the West, we can no longer think of economic progress as a necessary condition for population expansion. Because of the achievements of modern science, rapidly multiplying numbers are the rule even in countries where poverty for the existing masses remains the outstanding fact of economic life.

---

[1] This is not to say that *all* the effects of economic development in these countries were in the direction of producing rapid population growth. In order to analyze this question, we would have to take into account the effect of development not only on the *death-rate* but on the *birth-rate* as well. In point of fact, there is a good deal of evidence to suggest that economic development—with its typical accompaniments of industrialization and urbanization—will often bring an eventual decline in the birth-rate. This was the case in the United States and many other industrial nations during the nineteenth and much of the twentieth centuries. (See below, p. 62.)

NATURAL RESOURCES

The modern population explosion is taking place in a world whose estimated surface area is 196,838,000 square miles. Of this, roughly 30 per cent (57,168,000 square miles) is land. Of the land area, in turn, roughly one-third is cultivable, the rest being in areas which are either too cold, too mountainous, too dry, or too lacking in soil to permit permanent cultivation. A good deal of the non-cultivable area is, however, productive in that it may be used for forests or for grazing and, of course, may be the source of important mineral deposits.

Table 1-2   CULTIVATION OF THE WORLD'S LANDS

Use of Land	Area (mill hectares *)	Percentage of Total Area
Arable or cropped	1,384	10.1
Permanent meadows and pastures	2,407	17.6
Forested lands	3,839	28.1
Other	6,040	44.2

* 1 hectare = 2.47 acres
Because of large areas of land which are too mountainous, dry, cold, or lacking in topsoil, well under half the world's surface is suitable for cultivation.

Source: Stamp, op. cit., p. 40.

Natural resources, like population and labor supply, necessarily play an important role in a country's economic development. An economy's output will depend significantly on the quantity and location of its soil, forests, fisheries, coal, iron, oil, water, and all the other materials, organic and inorganic, which technology may require. What can we say in a general way about the supply of land and natural resources available to an economy in the course of its economic development?

The simple answer to this question, at least as far as land is concerned, might seem to be that everything remains unchanged—i.e., that the supply available to the economy remains fixed over time. Indeed, in the past, economists used to define "land" in an economic sense as consisting of the "original and indestructible" powers of the soil. In this way, natural resources were contrasted with man on the one hand and man-made instruments of production on the other. Population may grow; tools, factories and machinery may be built; but our basic underlying resources remain given to us once and for all.

However, this view of the matter has proved unsatisfactory for a variety of reasons. For one thing, it is clear that there is very little that is "indestructible" about natural resources. This is obviously true of mineral resources, which can be depleted or exhausted. It is equally true of forests, which can be cut down without adequate replacement. It is also true of the soil itself, which may lose its fertility as a result of unsatisfactory methods of cultivation. In Africa today, for example, there are many areas where over-grazing, destruction of brush by fire, and improper systems of rotation have resulted in wholesale degradation of the soil. In Latin America, it is estimated that a quarter of the total land which is or has been cultivated has lost its topsoil through erosion. In the United States, the cause of "conservation," which has attracted so many enthusiastic adherents from the day of Teddy Roosevelt on, is itself testimony to the "destructibility" of the gift of Nature.

An equally important qualification to the picture of unchanging resources lies in the fact that the process of economic development has often and, in fact, has typically resulted in the discovery and opening up of new resources. An unknown resource, though it may have been there all along, is of no economic significance whatever. Moreover, even if they are known, resources must be made accessible. To discover that the crust of a distant planet contains large quantities of a precious mineral is of little help if we lack the means to reach the planet and carry its treasure back to earth. Insofar as a country's economic progress is associated with the location, opening up, and utilization of additional resources, then, the economically effective supply has been increased.

How significant is this factor? In the past its significance is difficult to over-estimate. Much of the history of Western civilization can be written in terms of the acquisition of land and resources, including among other things, the discovery of the New World. Moreover, among the countries with the world's highest living standards at the present time are the United States and Canada, in both of which the process of economic development and that of discovering, opening up, and utilizing new resources went hand in hand. Resource discovery, not only directly but also in more intangible ways, as, for example, when it is associated with the vigorous life of a "frontier," has unquestionably been a major factor in past economic development.

What the future role of resources discovery will be is, of course, much less certain. In the world as a whole, there are no longer any great virgin areas rich with resources waiting for the explorer and pioneer to tap them. It is true that discoveries are still being made. The recent finding of oil in Libya, a country which had previously been cited for the poverty of its resources, suggests that there remain a few surprises ahead of us. The discovery of oil or other minerals in Nigeria, Liberia, and Algeria are similar examples. Indeed, in most of the underdeveloped countries, the work of charting the underlying national resource endowment by means of systematic surveys is just now getting underway. In this respect, the process of economic development is leading to the effective acquisition of new resources in these countries, as it did in earlier times.

Still, common sense tells us that, for the foreseeable future, the increase in the world's supply of natural resources will have a different and far more limited role in economic development than in centuries past. Our planet is far better known and much more intensively utilized now than in the age of the great discoveries; and, as far as other planets are concerned, their promise, though perhaps real, is still very distant.

This does not mean, however, that we should henceforth accept the view of resources as something static, fixed and given. For the significant fact in a technologically changing world is that the nature of the resources which are vital is also changing constantly. The great growth of the petroleum industry, the revolution in synthetic materials, the development of nuclear energy—all these suggest technological changes which have effected or may effect a great transformation in our attitude regarding the importance of particular resources. Since man is constantly reacting to and attempting to make use of what he has (and not what he no longer has), a constant shifting in the composition of our economically significant resources can be expected to take place over the indefinite future. A scarcity of resources can limit a country's economic development; but we must not underestimate man's capacity for "creating" resources by creating new uses for them.

CAPITAL ACCUMULATION

The third major factor of production, besides labor and land [2] is capital. Capital may be defined as follows :

> A country's capital is its stock of produced or man-made means of production, consisting of such items as buildings, factories, machinery, tools, equipment and inventories of goods in stock.

Since the term "capital" is often used in a variety of different senses, a few comments about this definition should be made.

In the first place, you will notice that we have defined capital in terms of tangible physical goods and not, as the word is sometimes employed, to cover money, or bonds, stocks, and other securities. Financial, or "liquid," assets are very important in economic life but they are clearly different from the physical factor of production we have in mind.

Secondly, in order to distinguish capital from land and labor, we have spoken of it as being "produced" or "man-made." This is a very rough distinction at best. To give an important example: Suppose a man, instead of building an additional tool for his work, spends his time studying so that he

---

[2] The term "land" is often used in economics to cover not only land in the narrow sense but also natural resources generally. In reality, all these terms—labor, land, and capital—are very rough catchalls, covering a wide variety of more specific factors of production.

will be more skilled at using the tools he already has. Isn't this new skill as important as the additional tool? And hasn't this new "skilled labor" been "produced" in essentially the same way as more physical capital? In truth, the distinction is more for convenience than for anything else. Thus, in this case, as we shall have many occasions to stress, there is, in every society, a very important kind of *intangible capital*—its accumulated stock of knowledge, skills, and know-how—which may play quite as important a role in economic development as its more palpable twin.

Finally, we should notice that we have referred to capital as a *stock* of goods rather than as a *flow* of production over time. In order to discuss a *flow* of anything, we must specify the time period over which we are measuring it. A *stock* of something, however, is the amount of it which we have at a particular moment of time. The amount of food which a housewife has on her shelves at noon today is a *stock*. The amount of food her family consumed over the past week is a *flow*. Annual total output or output per capita are examples of economic *flows*. Capital, on the other hand, is the *stock* of buildings, tools, machinery, and so on, we have on hand at, say, 12 o'clock noon on some particular day.

Needless to say, this stock of capital may *change over time.* We may have more capital on hand at noon today than we did at noon a year ago today. And, in fact, it is this process of adding to our stock of capital over the years which is what we mean by *capital accumulation:*

> *Capital accumulation* is the process of adding to our stock of machinery, tools, buildings, etc., over time. If our stock of capital at the end of the year is larger than it was at the beginning, the difference represents the amount of capital we have accumulated during the year. Another name for this is *investment. Annual real investment* is the addition to our capital stock over the course of a year.

Capital accumulation and *investment,* then, are equivalent terms, and, in this real or physical sense, they both mean adding to our stock of produced means of production over time.

The importance of capital accumulation for increasing production has long been recognized by economists. This is a point which immediately comes home to anyone today who compares methods of production as between an underdeveloped and a developed country. Here is capital-poor agriculture in a village in northern India:

> Plowing, for example, was done with great labor using a three-inch point set in a wooden share. Irrigation required drawing up one bucket at a time: a week's labor by three men and two oxen was needed to irrigate a single acre of wheat. Sickles the size of a man's hand were used for harvesting all the grain, and the grain was threshed under the slow treading of the hooves of oxen.[3]

[3] McKim Marriott, "Technological Change in Overdeveloped Rural Areas," in Lyle W. Shannon, ed., *Underdeveloped Areas* (New York: Harper, 1957), p. 425.

11

By sharp contrast, here is capital-intensive agriculture in New Zealand, a developed country:

> Many a New Zealand dairyman never sees the milk he handles. Machine milkers transfer it from the cow by pipe to a tank truck, which transports it to the factory where it is pasteurized, tested for butterfat, and pooled into a general supply received by a factory, which may produce 35 tons of butter a day. The farmer works with mechanical appliances—trucks, tractors, electric fences, hay mowers, tedders, stackers, and ditchdiggers. On broken country, planes are used for fertilization and seeding by air and even for dropping fencing materials in high country.[4]

Capital accumulation is one of the main factors which sets off rich from poor countries in the modern age and the industrial era in general from the past history of the world.

Capital plays a many-sided role in increasing an economy's output. For one thing, it is closely related to the possibilities of effecting changes in the scale or technology of production. By adding to the stock of capital, an economy may be better able to enjoy the advantages of large-scale production and increased specialization. Capital accumulation is similarly the handmaiden of technological progress. The New Zealand dairyman's machine milkers represent an innovation in dairy farming, but if the farmer had not found the necessary capital in the form of the actual machines the innovation would have had no economic impact whatever.

Secondly, capital accumulation is necessary to outfit a growing population with the tools and implements of production. With the world's population increasing as it has been over the past century and as it will be increasing even more rapidly over the next, capital accumulation is indispensable for expanding production and providing employment for the growing labor force. If, with such increasing populations, net capital investment were to cease, countries would soon run out of physical facilities for employing their laborers. Factories might go to 2 or even 3 shifts, but they could hardly go to 4 or 5. There would be 10, 12, ultimately even 20 or 30 men to each shovel, screwdriver, or wrench. Under such circumstances men would soon be reduced to producing goods with inefficient methods and tools and, in reality, many men would not find employment at all and would constitute a drag on the productive members of the society.

Thirdly, and by the same principle, capital accumulation, if it is rapid enough, may lead to an *increased* supply of tools and machinery per worker. All sorts of jobs that workers used to do by hand they might now perform with the aid of various instruments and mechanical devices. Or, to put it another way, they might be able to use increasingly *indirect* or *roundabout*

[4] John B. Condliffe, "New Zealand," in Adamantios Pepelasis, Leon Mears, and Irma Adelman, eds., *Economic Development* (New York: Harper, 1961), p. 580.

methods of production.[5] By devoting time and labor to the production of more capital goods, output per laborer will be increased. Even in the absence of technological change, there are few societies where the addition of more capital per worker would not have the effect of raising output per capita substantially over long periods of time.

These, then, are some of the reasons why capital accumulation plays such an important role in promoting economic development. The next question, of course, is: What are the major factors which influence a society's rate of capital accumulation? Why do some societies invest a larger proportion of their production in capital formation than others? Why does a society increase its rate of capital accumulation?

These are among the most interesting and complex questions in the whole field of economic development, and we shall be discussing them again and again in the chapters to follow. The difficulty of making any general statement is indicated by the simple fact that even the mechanism by which a society accumulates capital may be very different from one country to another. Thus, in the Soviet Union, it is the state which determines what the rate of capital formation will be. In a Western "capitalistic" society the decisions are made by private individuals or, more likely, by some mixture of public and private agencies. For this reason, it can often happen that two countries at the same general stage of economic development may accumulate capital at quite different rates simply because they operate under different economic systems.[6]

There is, however, one aspect of the process of capital accumulation that has significance for all societies, and this is the fact that the accumulation of capital has certain economic costs as well as advantages. Suppose, for

---

[5] It was the great nineteenth-century Austrian economist, Böhm-Bawerk, who particularly emphasized the productivity of these roundabout or (to use still another name) *time-consuming* methods of production. A hypothetical example: A fisherman in a society that has no capital may have to wade out into the water and catch fish with his hands. After some capital accumulation has taken place, he will be able to use a spear or hand-net. Eventually, if more and more investments are made, he will end up with a fishing boat and large fishing nets and all the apparatus we associate with a commercial fisherman. Instead of fishing *directly* (with his hands), he uses *a roundabout, time-consuming* method (he must take time to construct the boat and the nets before he can use them). As a result, his daily haul of fish will be greatly increased, even making allowance for the labor he has had to spend accumulating his stock of tools. In short, according to Böhm-Bawerk, there is a *net* gain in productivity as a result of using such time-consuming methods. We get more fish in the long run as a result of taking time to make some implements than if we had devoted that same amount of time to wading into the water, and continuing to fish with our bare hands in a direct, non-capitalistic way.

[6] The reader should notice that the term *capitalism* for Western-type economies is really a misnomer. The accumulation and use of capital is equally important under Western or communist economic systems. What is really at stake is the method of accumulation and of ownership—whether in the hands of private individuals or the state. In both cases, capital itself is essential.

example, that a society is employing its resources to produce a certain output during a given year. Given this flow of output, the society now faces a choice: It can either consume all the output during the year (Eat, drink, and be merry!), or it can divert part of the flow into investment (A penny saved is a penny earned!). By investing, or adding to the capital stock, the society will be able to produce a higher output in future years. The *cost* is represented by the fact that if the people had not invested this output they would have been able to consume it. They have to give up present consumption in order to secure a higher level of output in the future. The process of capital accumulation therefore typically involves a choice between today's consumption and tomorrow's output, between today's comfort and tomorrow's economic growth. The way in which a society makes this choice will clearly have a marked effect on its economic development.[7]

SPECIALIZATION, DIVISION OF LABOR, LARGE-SCALE PRODUCTION

Population growth, the opening up of new resources, and the accumulation of capital can all contribute substantially to the growth of an economy's output. If, however, society had to rely solely on the increase in its factors of production—that is, without undergoing basic changes in the organization and techniques of production— it is doubtful that the phenomenon of economic development as we have known it during the past 200 years would ever have taken place. It has been characteristic of this development wherever it has occurred that total output has grown far more rapidly than can be accounted for by an increase in the factors of production alone. In any listing of the elements affecting economic growth, therefore, we must leave an important place for those which involve changes in the way we use our factors of production.

One such set of changes has to do with increases in the scale and specialization of production.[8] If we were to go back in time, say to medieval

---

[7] Even this general point needs a qualification. If a society has unemployed resources, it may be able to increase *both* consumption and investment at the same time— i.e., by putting these idle resources to work. Thus, for example, the United States was able to expand war production rapidly in the early years of World War II without any major production sacrifice of consumption because of the backlog of unemployed labor from the Depression. Many observers believe that most underdeveloped countries have unemployed resources which could, if effectively mobilized, be used in this way.

[8] Changes in scale and changes in specialization are not the same things, though they often go together in fact. By changes in *scale* we mean primarily changes in the size of the basic production units, or firms, which make up the economy. Increasing *specialization*, on the other hand, refers to the subdividing of the production process into its component parts which are then handled by specialized machinery or labor. In general, a large firm is probably more easily able to employ specialized methods than a very small one. At the same time, it sometimes happens that when the production process is broken down into its component elements, a particular firm may concentrate solely on

Europe, one of the first things to strike us would be the very small size of the typical industrial enterprise and the lack of any detailed differentiation of productive functions. Such industry as there was was carried out in craft shops in the towns or, very frequently, as a simple adjunct to an agricultural way of life on the medieval estates. The peasant serf not only tilled the fields but also repaired his plow and built his hut and furniture; his wife and daughters did the baking, spinning, and weaving. In a few industries there did occur certain early examples of large-scale production, but these were the exception rather than the rule. Even in the urban areas, where the crafts were more clearly delineated, the typical shop was a small one, employing, besides the master, only 3 or 4 journeymen or apprentices; the total number of workers seldom reached as high as 10. In such a world, specialization, or the "division of labor" as it is sometimes called, was necessarily limited.

In the modern industrialized world, all this has been changed. Production is often on a large, sometimes on a massive, scale. In the United States there are several dozen corporations with assets of over $1 billion each. In many important industries 3 or 4 firms dominate our huge national and international markets. In these large firms, assembly-line and conveyor-belt techniques often bring an infinitely minute division of labor, as typified in the standard caricature of the worker who does nothing all day but turn a single bolt on a passing piece of mechanism. Specialization at higher levels involves the expertise of the scientist, engineer, and technician. The frequent criticism of the modern age—that it produces "narrow specialists" rather than well-rounded human beings—is a symptom of the degree to which this form of productive organization has come to dominate our lives.

Why does increasing specialization lead to increasing productivity? The answer to this question was given by Adam Smith, the great Scottish philosopher and political economist, whose *Wealth of Nations* (1776) has often been considered the foundation of modern economics. Smith took up the matter in the very first chapter of his classic work when he observed: "The greatest improvement in the productive powers of labour and the greater part of the skill, dexterity, and judgment with which it is any where directed, or applied, seem to have been the effects of the division of labour."

To prove his contention, Smith gave an example of a pin factory. If one man alone tried to make pins, he argued, he would be lucky if he managed to turn out a few crooked pins a day working at top speed. If, however, the number of men employed is increased, then it will be possible to divide the functions of pin-making among them: "one man draws out the wire, another straights it, a third cuts it, a fourth points it, a fifth grinds it at the top for receiving the head," and so on. According to Smith, the result of this

---

some very narrow aspect of production—turning out possibly only a single special part or piece of equipment. In such cases, a high degree of specialization and relatively small firms are quite compatible.

increased division of labor would be: (a) Each worker would become far more efficient at his task since he is now concentrating his full efforts on it; (b) there would be less time lost in shifting from one kind of work to another; and (c) each worker, knowing his job so well, would be more likely to think up new and better ways of performing it efficiently (including inventing machinery to save himself work). The final consequence would be the production of thousands of perfect pins, an increase in output far beyond anything which could be accounted for by the simple increase in the number of laborers employed.

Adam Smith's arguments are still valid today, and we can only underline his conception of the potential economic gains of increased scale and specialization. By enabling an economy to utilize individual skills and special regional or geographic advantages; by developing increased competence and expertise; by facilitating the mechanization and standardization of production —such changes in the organization of industry can contribute powerfully to economic growth.

Besides calling attention to these factors, Adam Smith also provided an important insight into the conditions which might produce them. Division of labor, he wrote in a significant statement, is limited by the "extent of the market." In a small island economy cut off from the world, there would be no need for the thousands of pins which even a small pin factory could produce, and certainly no place for a modern corporation. If such a society needed pins, it would doubtless produce them on a smaller scale and with less specialization of labor and machinery and, consequently, at a greater cost in terms of labor, land, and capital per unit of product. Thus, it is only as the market is expanded that an economy can take full advantage of these potential cost reductions.

The "extent of the market," in turn, depends on many factors. For one thing, it requires an economy that is in the habit of producing goods for exchange and not simply for home consumption. In the medieval world, where the vast majority of the population of Europe lived on relatively isolated rural estates, the possibilities of exchange were very limited and much production was dictated by the requirements of local self-sufficiency.

For another, it depends on the adequacy of transport and communications in bringing the various sectors of the economy together. In our own country, as late as 1812, it took 115 days and a freight cost of $1,000 to transport a wagonload of goods overland from Maine to Georgia. Geographic size does not create a large market if the crucial transport links are missing.

Moreover, the "extent of the market" will also typically depend on the general level of the production within the market area. This may be a particularly important point in many underdeveloped countries today, where the average worker's productivity is so extremely low. Imagine, for example, a country where the average level of output per capita is $75 or $100 per year. In such a poverty-stricken economy, the "extent of the market" for such commodities as automobiles, consumer appliances, and industrial products would be very limited. At best, the effective market for these products would be restricted to a small group of wealthy individuals. For the mass of the population, necessity would require that the great bulk of productive effort be directed toward food and a minimum of clothing and shelter. Under such circumstances large-scale industry might have a difficult time finding buyers even in the most heavily populated areas.

In short, in order to investigate the potentialities of increasing scale and specialization in any particular context, we would have to look closely at all those factors bearing on the growth and character of the markets available. The spread of exchange relationships, improvements in transport, population growth, the level of output per capita—all these factors, and others, will determine whether or not a society will be able to enjoy the "improvement in the productive powers of labour" which Adam Smith saw as central to economic progress.

TECHNOLOGICAL PROGRESS

One last factor completes our list—technological progress. We arrive here at what is perhaps the greatest single distinguishing characteristic of the modern age. It is by now a commonplace that technology is revolutionizing our lives. Through new techniques and methods of production, an economy is enabled to produce commodities at a fraction of their former cost in terms of the amount of land, labor, and capital devoted to their production. Equally significantly, technology constantly brings forth a flood of new products which no amount of effort and resources could have produced in the past. If the modern industrial nations are often criticized for their impersonal specialization, they are even more frequently condemned for having become the slaves of gadgets and appliances. This is a deep and important question concerning the values we choose to live by. For good or for ill, however, economic growth draws its vital nourishment from a stream of fresh ideas, inventions, devices, and techniques without which—no matter how favorable all other factors might have been—modern development would have been essentially inconceivable.

Technological progress is not, of course, a new phenomenon in human history. Over a period of hundreds of thousands of years, mankind succeeded in making a number of epochal technological advances which compare favorably in their impact with anything the modern age has to offer. The use of objects as tools, the control of fire, the invention of the wheel, the domestication of plants and animals, the making of pottery, the use of bronze, the introduction of iron—all these represent technological progress of the most fundamental kind. What *is* unique about the modern era, however, is the rapidity, depth, and constancy of the flow of new technology. Past progress— **17** like past economic development in general—was sporadic, uneven, and slow. Now, and increasingly as the years go by, technological progress has become systematic and dependable; and it comes not in a trickle but in a flood.

Technological progress in this modern sense depends, of course, on applied science and ultimately on pure science. Abstract speculations on the nature of the universe, motivated originally by the simple desire to know and understand, will often later come to roost in some practical appliance which reduces labor or provides for hitherto unsuspected needs. In a certain sense, the "scientific attitude" is at the root of the whole thing. The notion of a rational and comprehensible universe, of natural laws which can be apprehended and manipulated, of systematic, objective methods which can be used to unlock nature's secrets—this kind of approach is by no means a necessary or universal one, and, in fact, was the product of a long process of intellectual evolution in the Western World.

The progress of science also depends, however, on the resources which are applied to scientific effort. This may be particularly true in the areas of applied science and technology. Thus, education is a factor of central importance. An illiterate society is unlikely to be in the forefront of technological creativity nor for that matter to know how to *use* new technologies even if they exist for the taking. How, for example, is a country like Indonesia to participate in the general technological revolution when 90 per cent or more of the population can neither read nor write? Furthermore, as development proceeds, the demand for highly trained technicians and specialists constantly increases.

This new emphasis on education as a factor in economic growth has brought forth in very recent years a rapidly growing literature on such questions as: How does the rate of economic return on education as an investment compare with the rate of return on physical capital? How is the volume of educational expenditures correlated with a country's level or rate of growth of national output? What part of a country's economic growth can reasonably be attributed to its educational effort? These are highly difficult questions, but also highly important ones.[9]

Besides education, rapid technological change also characteristically requires some business leaders who will introduce the new technology, or as they are commonly called, *entrepreneurs*. To put it in technical terms, it is important to recognize that there is a need not only for *invention* but also for *innovation,* or actually getting the new methods adopted in practically effective ways. Richard Arkwright, one of the great "cotton lords" of late eighteenth-century England, did not originate and may have stolen some of the basic inventions he patented, but he did introduce these devices commercially, employed them on a large scale, made a fortune for himself, and

[9] For a useful general study of this range of questions, see F. Harbison and C. Myers, *Education, Manpower and Economic Growth* (New York: McGraw-Hill, 1964).

was one of the key figures in the launching of the English industrial revolution.

Once we broaden our view of technological progress to include the whole process of *innovation,* we begin to see just how complex this matter is. New techniques, to be economically effective, may require additional capital, changes in the scale of enterprise, and a trained and disciplined labor force. In an even deeper sense, they may require a society which is willing and able to adjust itself to economic *change.* Until modern times, economic change has always been a very gradual process. In most societies, attitudes and institutions are necessarily geared not to what is new but to what is traditional. The very *idea* of progress is strictly a modern phenomenon.

The subject is as fascinating as it is difficult. What kind of a society is it that produces a Richard Arkwright? a Henry Ford? If the religious or ethical values of a society preclude material gain as a proper goal of conduct, will such individuals be able to emerge? Can the state, as in the modern Soviet Union, take over the entrepreneurial functions which in other societies are largely reserved for private parties?

Such questions make abundantly clear that the subject of economic development ultimately involves not only economics but also history, sociology, perhaps even philosophy. And this is really to be expected since development is a human enterprise and one that reaches to the very roots of our social organization.

WEIGHTING FACTORS
AND THE "RESIDUAL"

The foregoing comments will make it clear that any attempt to assign relative *quantitative* weights to the various factors in development we have discussed would be fraught with difficulties. Nevertheless, unless such assessments are made, there can be no real progress toward a deeper understanding of the development process. Aware of this fact, economists in the last decade have made intensive and sometimes elaborate efforts to compare quantitatively the contributions various factors have made to economic growth.

These studies have been largely limited to economically advanced countries and they have characteristically divided the sources of growth into three elements: growth in the labor force, growth in capital, and a third term, sometimes called "technical progress," which is really a "residual" item once the contributions of labor and capital have been estimated. This "residual" clearly covers more than what we have called technological progress since, for example, increasing returns to scale would be subsumed here as, indeed, would variations in the quality of the labor and capital employed by the society. It is then something of a catch-all, although the

19

emphasis is clearly on the organization, utilization, and quality of the society's factors of production as opposed to the mere increase in the quantity of those factors.

One way to make such calculations is to say that technical change is equal to the percentage growth in output over a given time period divided by a term representing the percentage increase in labor and capital.

> In a simple case, suppose that labor and capital are both increasing at 2 per cent per year and that total output is increasing at 4 per cent per year. In this case it is clear that output is increasing more rapidly than are the factor inputs and, indeed, a reasonable estimate of the rate of technical change would be in the vicinity of 2 per cent per year. If labor and capital are increasing at different rates, the problem becomes more complex—since some method must be found for weighting the labor and capital elements—but the fundamental idea is the same.[10]

In this way, or in other more complicated ways, economists have been attempting to assign priorities to the various elements in the growth process.

The major result of these several studies has been to suggest the very great importance of technological progress or, more accurately, the "residual" element in the growth process. We shall be returning to this matter in our analysis of economic growth in the United States in Chapter 4, but the general drift of much of this new analysis can be indicated by the results shown in Table 1-3. The time period of this particular study is fairly short (no more than a dozen years) and the method of weighting is necessarily fairly rough; still, the importance of the "residual" element is quite clear. In no case does it account for less than 30 per cent of the observed growth rate and, in one case, it accounts for half. If we were to go further into the matter and ask the question: What percentage of the growth in output per laborer in these countries during these periods should be attributed to the fact that the laborer has more capital to work with and what percentage to the fact that there has been "technical progress," we should get even higher percentages in the latter column.

[10] In the case where capital and labor are increasing at different rates, each might be weighted by its relative share of national income, thus giving a rough sense of its importance in the national economy. The subject, however, is very complex and the interested student must work his way through the relevant literature. This would include such works as: Robert M. Solow, "Technical Change and the Aggregate Production Function," *Review of Economics and Statistics,* Vol. XXXIX, No. 3 (August, 1957); Moses Abramowitz, "Resource and Output Trends in the United States Since 1870," National Bureau of Economic Research, Occasional Paper No. 52 (1956); Solomon Fabricant, "Basic Facts on Productivity Change," National Bureau of Economic Research, Occasional Paper No. 63 (1959); John W. Kendrick, *Productivity Trends in the United States* (Princeton: Princeton University Press, 1961); Edward F. Denison, *Sources of Economic Growth in the United States* (Committee for Economic Development, Supplementary Paper No. 13, January, 1962). For a recent (but not easy) survey of this field, Lester B. Lave, *Technological Change; Its Conception and Measurement* (Englewood Cliffs, N.J.: Prentice-Hall, 1966).

Table 1-3 THE "RESIDUAL" IN ECONOMIC GROWTH

Country	Period	Annual Percentage Rate of Growth		Ratio Between Annual Rates of Growth of "Residual" and Output in Percentages
		Output	"Residual"	
U.S.	1948-60	3.4	1.4 *	47
Canada	1949-60	4.0	1.2	30
U.K.	1949-59	2.4	.6	25
Germany	1950-59	7.4	3.6	50
Japan	1951-59	8.4	3.7	44

* Private economy

Source: E. Domar, S. M. Eddie, B. Herrick, P. Hohenberg, M. Intriligator, I. Miyamoto, "Economic Growth and Productivity in the United States, Canada, United Kingdom, Germany and Japan in the Post-War Period," The Review of Economics and Statistics, Vol. XLVI, (February, 1964), No. 1.

In short, modern growth must always be thought of not merely as increases in the factor inputs but as radical and continuing change in the mode of utilizing those factors. It depends not only on labor and capital hours, but on the skill, quality, knowledge, and attitudes of the human beings who give modern development its shape and direction.

SUMMARY

In this chapter we have set out in summary form some of the general factors which underlie the process of economic development. These factors can be thought of in terms of increases in a society's basic factors of production—labor, land, and capital—and/or improvements in the organization and technology by which these factors of production are employed. The subjects covered were:

Population growth. An increasing population means more labor but also more mouths to feed; its effects on economic development will depend on such things as the pattern of population growth, the expansion of markets it brings, and the pressure it creates on scarce natural resources and the stock of capital.

Natural resources. Natural resources cannot be considered a fixed constraint on economic development; resources may be "used up," additional resources may be discovered or acquired, and, finally, different resources may be taken up as technology progresses.

Capital accumulation. Capital accumulation facilitates the introduction of new technology, provides tools for a growing population, and brings about

21

the use of productive "roundabout" processes; the cost of capital accumulation is the output we could have consumed today but have invested for higher outputs tomorrow.

Scale, specialization, division of labor. By introducing larger-scale production units with increased specialization and "division of labor," a society is able to get more output from its given factors of production; the possibility of using such methods is greatly affected by the "extent of the market."

Technological progress. Technological progress brings basic changes in productive techniques and new products; it depends on the progress of science, on the level of education in the society, and, in terms of practical innovations, upon the existence of strong *entrepreneurship* in the society.

Recent years have brought attempts by economists to give quantitative weight to these various growth factors. Dividing these factors into the categories of labor, capital, and a "residual" item called "technical progress," economists have discovered the rather striking contribution of the last term. These studies, though still preliminary in nature, strongly suggest that modern growth is not simply increases in the society's factors of production, but involves significant changes in the way those factors of production are utilized.

Approaches

to the Theory of Development

In the last chapter, we surveyed some of the major factors underlying the process of economic development and indicated some recent attempts to give weight to these factors. These steps are important to our inquiry, but they are necessarily only a beginning. We want to know how these factors are inter-related, why they are strong and vigorous in one context and weak and ineffectual in another, how they produce (or fail to produce) the phenomenon of modern economic growth by their manifold actions and reactions. The attempt to answer such questions—to formulate the general conditions under which growth will or will not occur—is the task of a theory of economic development.

THE "STAGES"
OF ECONOMIC GROWTH

The search for such a theory has occupied the attention of economists at one time or another ever since the English industrial revolution of the eighteenth century made the phenomenon of rapid and persistent growth an economic reality.

One approach, sometimes more descriptive than theoretical, has attempted to categorize the growth process in terms of various "stages" through which all countries will pass in their natural economic evolution. Thus, for example, some economic historians in the past have tried to define the "stages" of development in terms

23

of the manner in which the market and exchange mechanisms of a society operated. Countries were seen as following a more or less regular pattern from a "barter economy" to a "money economy" and then, finally, to a "credit economy."

More recently, economists have focused a good deal of attention on the nature of the productive activities in which a society is engaged. Economic development, it has been noticed, is regularly accompanied by an increase in the percentage importance of industry relative to agriculture. The modern British economist, Colin Clark, goes further and asserts that there are really three stages involved: (1) In underdeveloped societies, agriculture is the dominant occupation and source of income. (2) As the society develops, manufacturing industry grows relative to agriculture. Finally, (3) as the economy becomes still more developed, it is the "tertiary," or service, industries which show the greatest rate of advance.[1]

The attempt to analyze the development process through such "stages" often brings out important "uniformities" linking together otherwise quite dissimilar situations. At the same time, most of these theories have had to cope with a certain number of exceptions; and, in general, they tend to tell us more about what happened than exactly why and how it happened.

There was, however, one theory which purported not only to find a succession of stages through which an economy must pass but also to give a full-scale analysis of the mechanisms by which this evolution was accomplished. This was the theory of Karl Marx.

Marx found his key factor in the control of the society's basic means of production and the mechanism of change in the "class struggle." As he wrote in the *Communist Manifesto* (1848):

> The history of all hitherto existing societies is the history of class struggles. Freeman and slave, patrician and plebeian, lord and serf, guild-master and journeyman, in a word, oppressor and oppressed, stood in constant opposition to one another, carried on an uninterrupted, now hidden, now open fight, a fight that ended, either in a revolutionary re-constitution of society at large, or in the common ruin of the contending classes.

Though this theory was designed to embrace all past societies, Marx's particular interest was in the process by which the "capitalist" stage would inevitably lead to the (final) stage of communism. His analysis was complex but it involved the notion of a continuing exploitation of labor—the "proletariat"—by the entrenched capitalistic classes. Labor was never paid its full value. If wages threatened to rise, capitalists replaced labor with machinery, thus creating a large body of unemployed whose existence kept wages down. At the same time, the capitalist himself was facing difficulties. Since profits, according to Marx, derived ultimately from the work of laborers, the more the

[1] For Clark's theory, see his *Conditions of Economic Progress,* 3rd ed. (London: Macmillan, 1957).

workers were replaced by machinery the harder it was for the capitalist to maintain his rate of profit. This pressure led to increasing exploitation of the proletariat, more unemployment, mass misery and, finally, the revolution. Communism was thus seen as the end-product of the last stages of capitalism when the increasing impoverishment of the proletariat led the masses to unite to throw off their chains!

No one in the modern world needs be reminded how influential the writings of Karl Marx have been. Moreover, his writings have had most appeal in those areas of the world where the pursuit of economic growth has been most intense. Thus, it was in backward Russia in 1917, in poverty-stricken China after World War II, and in countless other poor and upward-striving countries where he has had his greatest triumphs. For millions of people, Marx has provided the ideological banner under which they hope to match and ultimately overtake the economies of the industrialized West.

At the same time, the Marxian theory provides a poor framework for trying to understand the kind of problems we are concerned with. Marxian analysis, as we have suggested, came to the conclusion that the capitalistic system would inevitably lead to the impoverishment of the masses and that the revolution which would usher in communism would come as the end-product of capitalistic development. In point of fact, neither of these predictions is supported by subsequent historical experience. One of the most outstanding features of development in the West has been the extraordinary improvement in the conditions of the laboring classes; and, as far as revolutions are concerned, they have taken place not, as Marx would have expected, in the advanced, capitalistic societies, but in the poor, relatively underdeveloped countries, many of which have hardly gone through the capitalistic stage at all. Thus, while we must recognize the extraordinary impact of his works and also the many important particular insights he developed, we would find Marx a rather misleading guide to the growth process as we have actually observed it.[2]

THE "CLASSICAL" THEORY

Another early theory that requires mention is what is sometimes called the "classical" theory of economic development. This theory was the product of a school of late-eighteenth and early-nineteenth century British economists who followed in the wake of Adam Smith—notably, Thomas Robert Malthus and David Ricardo. In a certain sense, the "classical" pre-

[2] A modern attempt to "answer" Marx with a set of non-Marxian "stages" is given by W. W. Rostow in his book, *The Stages of Economic Growth* (London: Cambridge University Press, 1960). We shall be referring to Rostow's work later in this chapter but not to his 5-stage sequence, which, from the point of view of historical evidence, seems fairly debatable. For a much more detailed discussion of some of the theories taken up in this chapter, especially Marxian theory and the "classical" theory mentioned in the next section, see, in this Series, my *Evolution of Modern Economics*.

dictions of the future were as faulty or even more faulty than the later predictions of Marx, but they did isolate a problem which has striking relevance to certain areas of the modern world.

In terms of the factors we discussed in the last chapter, the "classical" economists put their primary emphasis on population growth and natural resources. In its simplest form, their theory was based on two propositions: (1) that a country's population will invariably increase whenever the standard of living rises above some minimum "subsistence" level; and (2) that any increase in population will bring "diminishing returns" to labor because of the scarcity of agricultural land.

As far as the first proposition is concerned, Malthus and Ricardo seem to have believed that improved economic conditions would both lower the death-rate (less hunger and better health) and raise the birth-rate (earlier marriages and more children). The "subsistence" level thus has some of the properties of a *biological* minimum, or the income necessary for physical survival, and of a more *conventional* minimum, or the level people consider socially necessary for marrying and raising families.

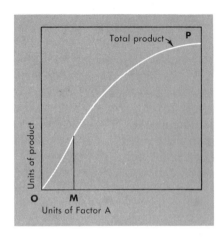

FIG. 2-1 Law of diminishing returns.

Their second proposition is a special application of a famous and still generally accepted "law" of economics—i.e. the *law of diminishing returns*. This law states that in the production of any commodity, as we add more units of one factor of production to a fixed quantity of another factor (or factors), the addition to total product with each subsequent unit of the variable factor will eventually begin to diminish. Figure 2-1 shows how total product increases as we add more units of factor of production *A* when other factors (*B, C,* etc.) are held constant.[3] At the *very* beginning (up to *OM* units of factor *A*), "returns" are in-

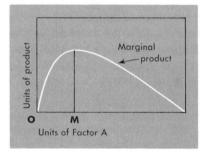

[3] Using Fig. 2-1 as our reference, we could also draw a curve of the *marginal product* of factor *A*. This curve would show rising marginal product up to *OM* units of factor *A* and a declining marginal product thereafter. If total product ceased to rise at all as more units of factor *A* were applied, we would get a zero-marginal product, a case we shall discuss presently.

creasing—i.e. each successive unit of the factor adds more to total product than did the previous units. After *OM,* however, the law of diminishing returns begins to apply. What is actually diminishing is the *addition* to total product with each successive unit of *A,* or what economists call the *marginal product* of factor *A.*

In the particular case of the "classical" economists, they took agricultural land to be the essentially fixed factor and thought of labor as the factor which might (unless checked) increase indefinitely. Their description of the effects of an increase in population can be summarized as follows: An increased population brings an increased demand for food. The increased demand for food means, in turn, that we have either: (1) to bring new agricultural land under cultivation or (2) to use additional labor in a more intensive cultivation of land already under plow. Given the over-all limitation of land supply, any new land which we bring into cultivation will be inferior in quality to the land already in use. (Why inferior? Because we wouldn't have been using inferior lands earlier when superior lands were available, and there is a limitation on the total amount of superior land.) On the other hand, if we practice more intensive cultivation on the good land, each laborer on the average has less land to work with. In either case, then, we get the same result. Food production will ultimately grow less rapidly than population.

Once these two propositions are accepted, the general lines of development in the "classical" style become quite clear. Suppose that in some early stage of society economic conditions are favorable, wages are high, people generally are living comfortably. What will happen? According to the first proposition, population will begin to increase. People will be healthy and well; early marriages and large families will be the order of the day.

But now, with the population increase, diminishing returns begins to take its toll. The food supply does not grow as rapidly as the number of people. Little by little, living standards will begin to fall. How long will they continue to fall? Essentially until population growth finally comes to a halt. And when will population growth come to a halt? Only when, according to the theory, the general standard of living has fallen to some very low "subsistence" level.

The ultimate destination of the "natural progress" of an economy, therefore, is a state in which the country generally has been reduced to a kind of economic minimum. Moreover, this state tends to preserve itself. With living standards at the "subsistence" level, population neither increases nor decreases. The number of people and the available resources are in balance. A "stationary" situation has been achieved—and, of course, at a level of general poverty.

LABOR SURPLUS THEORIES

The "classical" theory turned out to be a rather poor description of what actually happened to the British economy in the nineteenth century, but it was rediscovered in the twentieth century as indicating a major problem of the modern underdeveloped countries. Indeed, population pressures are characteristic of so many of these countries that a number of present-day theorists have been attempting to analyze development in the context of what is sometimes called a "labor surplus" economy.[4]

These new theories characteristically conceive the underdeveloped economy as operating in two sectors: (1) a traditional agricultural sector, and (2) a much smaller and also more modern industrial sector. "Labor surplus" means the existence of such a large population in the rural sector that the marginal product of labor has fallen to zero. Laborers may appear to be doing work of one sort or another but they are so crowded on the land that if some of the labor were removed total product would remain unchanged. This condition is also called *disguised unemployment* and is differentiated from the more open unemployment to be found in the cities of underdeveloped countries.

The essence of the development process in this kind of economy is the transfer of labor resources from the agricultural sector, where they add nothing to production, to the more modern industrial sector, where they create a surplus that may be used for further growth and development. In the setting of a private or market economy, the process might evolve as follows. First of all, the laborers must be attracted from the agricultural to the industrial sphere. Presumably, they would have to be offered wages which somewhat exceed the incomes they would receive if they remained in agriculture. However, since productivity is low in the agricultural sector, these wages would still be quite low. Second, employers in the industrial sector would hire these laborers to the point where it ceased to be profitable to do so. Since the wage is low, they would be able to hire a not inconsiderable amount of labor in this more productive sector and thus gain a considerable surplus for themselves in the form of profits. Third, they would take some or all of these profits and reinvest them in capital equipment, machinery, buildings, and the like. It is, of course, possible that the employers might simply pocket the surplus but this would be fairly uncharacteristic behavior for industrial capitalists as, indeed, even Karl Marx recognized. Presuming that they do reinvest their profits, the effect of this third stage of the process will be to create the opportunity for further transfer of labor from the agricultural sector, of an additional surplus in industry, and, once again, of

[4] These new theories owe much to the path-breaking work of W. Arthur Lewis, in his article, "Economic Development with Unlimited Supplies of Labour," *Manchester School* (May, 1954). A recent and elaborate discussion of the labor surplus economy is given in John Fei and G. Ranis, *Development of the Labor Surplus Economy* (Homewood, Ill.: Irwin, 1964).

still further reinvestment in capital goods. The process, in other words, is on-going. When it is successful, the transfer of labor from agriculture to industry is rapid enough so that, even when population is growing, there is a progressively higher percentage of the labor force in the industrial sector.

When we come to a more detailed discussion of the modern under-developed countries, we shall see that there are many complications in the smooth functioning of the process we have described. Even in a preliminary way, however, we should notice that the whole thing will falter unless there is some progress not only in the industrial but also in the *agricultural* sector. If we think of the problem in terms of food, we can expect the transfer of labor from agriculture to industry to be accompanied by an increased demand for food since (a) the incomes of the laboring class as a whole have risen and presumably some part of this increase will be spent on food, and (b) population is presumably increasing and more food will be necessary to sustain the growing numbers of people. If there is no (or little) agricultural progress in these circumstances, the result is likely to be a rise in agricultural prices relative to industrial prices. This, in turn, will have the effect of raising the wage at which employers will be able to secure labor from agriculture for the industrial sector. And *this,* in its turn, will slow up or even choke off the whole development process. For if the employers in industry have to pay high wages, then they will be unable to absorb as much labor as before, they will have less surplus to work with, and consequently the reinvestment process will be hampered. This is not the only way, but it is an important way, in which a failure in the agricultural sector—a sector often neglected by countries desiring quick, modern, factory-style development—can seriously impair the chances for growth in the economy as a whole.

NEEDED: A GENERAL FRAMEWORK

The "classical" and "labor surplus" theories take us part of the way toward an explanation of modern development, but only a small way. They do not apply to most developed nations whose historical experience involved a rather different kind of population condition; nor do they apply very well to the underdeveloped countries today that are relatively under-populated. A similar reservation must be applied to the analysis of the "residual" discussed at the end of the preceding chapter. It takes us part of the way toward understanding growth, but not very far—at least not until the analysis has become much more advanced than it is at the moment.

What this means, in effect, is that there is currently no body of analysis that could accurately be called a *general theory* of development. What we have, rather, is a number of loosely related insights and hypotheses, some of which are fairly generally accepted by economists, others of which are **29** subject to keen debate. One aspect of the development process that has received particular attention during the past 10 or 15 years is the problem of "getting started" on the path of modern growth. Faced with a world in which some economies grow perpetually richer and others seem to stagnate in poverty, economists have asked what is special and important in the period of transformation. Can the vital characteristics of what historians have long called "industrial revolutions" be ascertained? Even in this area, there is considerable difference of opinion among students of the problem; still, the intensive discussions of the past decade have brought forth a number of concepts that will be useful to us as a point of departure in the chapters that follow. To these fundamental concepts (and, in some cases, unsettled problems) we now turn.

OBSTACLES TO GROWTH

Since rapid economic growth is an historical abnormality—occurring only in the past century or two and even then only in certain countries —any over-all approach to the development process must take some account of the obstacles to growth and, in general, of the persistence of economic stagnation. One concept that has attracted some attention is that of the *vicious circles of poverty,* the essential notion being that a country's poverty may itself be one of the major obstacles to its growth and development. Because it is poor, the country does not develop; because it does not develop, it remains poor.

Several lines of reasoning have been advanced to support this general view of the problem. Consider, for example, the problem of capital accumulation. One of the significant aspects of the process of capital accumulation is that it involves the sacrifice of present consumption for higher levels of future output. Part of the stream of current production is diverted from immediate needs and added to the stock of capital where it will contribute to higher productivity. This aspect of capital formation we have discussed in the preceding chapter.

The situation in an underdeveloped country is that the majority of the population is living at the margin of subsistence. The peasant tills the soil with a few crude tools and implements; methods are primitive and inefficient; in the best of times, he harvests a sufficient crop to keep himself and his family at the level of survival, and then there are the years of drought, famine, and epidemic when existence itself is threatened. The point is that, under such circumstances, the deferment of any substantial amount of current consumption in favor of saving and capital formation will necessarily be very difficult. Now *if* productivity on the peasant holdings could be increased, then, of course, such deferment might occur and capital could be accumulated. But this constitutes the vicious circle. For these improvements in productivity will typically require that peasants have more and better tools—i.e., more capital—to work with. Without capital accumulation, output and pro-

30

ductivity will remain low. With low output and productivity, there will be no substantial savings or capital formation.

This example is rather oversimplified and it is also subject to certain objections, which will help explain why some modern economists reject the concept of vicious circles and even the notion of development as overcoming a series of difficult "obstacles." [5] In reality, even in quite poor countries, there are typically some important potential sources of saving and investment. Europe in the Middle Ages was not so poor that it could not build its cathedrals. Ancient Egypt had its pyramids. Even in the poorest modern underdeveloped countries, moreover, we often find large expenditures on ceremonials and celebrations that could, at least in theory, be diverted to productive capital accumulation.[6] Nor should we forget that in *every* poor society, there are always some individuals—princes, lords, landowners, merchants—who live comfortably above subsistence and who could, if they would, provide increased investment for the economy. The very fact that all societies throughout history have been able to find the resources for costly wars proves that potentialities exist, and that the circle is not so closed as might at first sight appear.

Still, these considerations tend to mitigate rather than remove the problem, and, furthermore, we have touched on only one aspect of the problem. Suppose, to carry the matter further, that the wealthy few in our poor society decide to forsake their typically luxurious or war-like manner of life in order to save and invest productively in industry and agriculture. What will the result be? For one thing, they may be able to find surprisingly few outlets for investment which are profitable. In a poor agrarian economy with the bulk of the population living in isolated rural villages, the "extent of the market" is, as we know, likely to be very limited. Lack of transport alone may pose almost insuperable obstacles. Consider conditions in Africa:

> Bold red lines representing main roads on African maps often turn out to be more like tracks and are frequently impassable in the rainy season. On other maps the lines turn out to be future networks, not the present one, there being no roads at all where some are indicated. One questions the aptness of the term "road" for some routeways: those in Ethiopia have been described as the only roads where pedestrians overtake automobiles. . . .[7]

[5] One distinguished economist who feels that there has been too much talk of "obstacles" to development is A. O. Hirschman, author of *The Strategy of Economic Development* (New Haven: Yale University Press, 1958). Hirschman feels that the key shortage is decision-making ability and that, if this resource can be mobilized, many of the alleged obstacles to development will disappear. We shall touch on Professor Hirschman's views again later (p. 96).

[6] Thus, for example, it is estimated that in poverty-stricken modern India, something like 7 per cent of all rural expenditures go for such ceremonials as weddings, funerals, birth celebrations, and the like. Similarly, in pre-Communist China, it used to take about 35 piculs of rice (equal to more than a year's output for many of the poorer peasants) just to get a son married off.

[7] William A. Hance, *African Economic Development,* Council on Foreign Relations (New York: Harper, 1958), p. 116.

Given such conditions, what chance would any reasonably large-scale industry have of success? How would it get its supplies? How would it transport its products over a wide enough area to make the investment profitable?

This problem of investment outlets is, in fact, related to a whole group of "vicious circles." There is the "vicious circle of a limited market." Large-scale industry requires a big market. But in a poor country the "extent of the market" is bound to be small. It will remain small, moreover, until large-scale industry is somehow established. There is a related and more general "vicious circle of interdependent production." Specialized industry is interdependent industry. A firm must have not only markets in which to sell its products but also supplying industries to provide the tools and unfinished goods its productive activities require. How are we to establish any *one* industry when these other supplying industries have not yet come into existence? But if we cannot succeed in establishing some one particular industry, how will *any* industries ever come to be established?

Nor is this all. In reality, many of the deepest and most difficult problems arise in connection with the society's attitudes and institutions. How likely is it—we have to ask—that the wealthy few will really wish to give up their aristocratic pattern of life, invest their wealth, and enter into the bustle of commercial and industrial activity? In medieval Europe, trade was frowned upon, merchants were thought socially inferior, and the lending of money at interest was considered a religious sin. In many modern underdeveloped countries, certain occupations are felt to be beneath the upper classes and an educated man would often sooner go without work at all than dirty his hands in an unsuitable profession. In almost all poor societies, the outlook is likely to be adjusted not to growth and change but to tradition and stability. The values which make life endurable under conditions of general poverty may be precisely those values which pose obstacles to material progress.

These conditions are not merely hypothetical. Indeed, the experience of the 1950's and 1960's has been that economic development in the poor countries of the world is extremely difficult to achieve. Some idealists have been discouraged by the lack of progress; the realist knows that it is only to be expected given the very difficult problems these countries face.

SELF-SUSTAINING GROWTH

To make the problem of beginnings—of "getting started"—as sharp as possible, let us move immediately from this picture of a struggling poverty-stricken community to one of a country in which economic growth has already become the order of the day. According to many economists, economic growth creates the conditions, mechanisms, and attitudes which reinforce the factors making for growth. The development process thus becomes *self-sustaining.* Here are some possible reasons why.

1. *Expanding markets:* Economic growth means an expansion in output and this implies a continuous widening of the "extent of the market." Actually, the expansion of the market is likely to occur all the more rapidly in a growing economy because economic development will typically bring with it a vast improvement in transport and communications facilities. Whole regions of the economy can specialize as this network of communications spreads over the face of the nation. Expanding industries will find their expansion matched and facilitated by the growth of other industries which supply markets for their products and the tools and unfinished products they need. In general, the expansion of the economy as a whole will tend to facilitate the expansion of each of its sectors.[8] Increased division of labor and larger-scale production will bring further rises in output per capita— further growth!

2. *Capital accumulation:* A developing society, a few degrees removed from the conditions of bare subsistence living, can afford to save and invest a larger proportion of its output. Moreover (and perhaps even more significantly), it will have the mechanisms to do so. As in the case of the "labor surplus" theory we have discussed earlier, an expanding industry will more or less automatically provide the sources of capital for a continuing expansion of industry. Industry is growing; firms are making profits; these profits can be plowed back into the firms in the form of additional investment. This, in turn, will make for further expansion, profits, reinvestment of earnings, and so on. Industrial expansion is regularly creating surpluses and putting them at the disposal of those who are already engaged in industrial activity and thus are particularly likely to use them productively. In a meaningful sense, economic development is generating its own sources of capital as it goes along.

3. *Innovation and technological change:* It will be much easier to introduce technological change in a developing economy. Partly, this is simply a reflection of the important interaction between innovation and the other growth-creating factors. New technologies often require more capital and a larger scale of production, and thus anything which facilitates capital accumulation and expanding markets will also contribute to a higher rate of technological progress. But there are many other elements at work also. More will be spent on research and education in a developing economy. Just as expanding industries will be plowing back their profits into increased plant and equipment, so also will they be devoting greater resources to research and development projects. Through education, more scientists and

---

[8] We have here what are sometimes called "external economies." Because of expansion in *other* firms or industries, a particular firm or industry finds its economic situation improved. Many economists feel that such "external economies," when they occur, play a vital role in a country's economic development.

engineers will be trained and the labor force will become more skilled at the application of new technologies. In an even deeper sense, the whole philosophy of innovation, change, and material progress is likely to permeate the society and this will promote a continuing process of economic growth.

These, then, are some of the reasons why modern economists often think of the growth process as *self-sustaining*. Once under way, an economy will find the obstacles of development disappearing. "Classical" worries about scarce resources and diminishing returns will prove quite unnecessary. Growth will promote growth in an ever-ascending spiral of rising output per capita and living standards.

We have put the case for *self-sustaining* growth in bold terms; now we must pause to ask how well this rather idyllic picture of continuing development fits the facts. As in the case of the notion of vicious circles, we find many reasons for having reservations about a too-simple view of the matter.

For one thing, it should be said that this hypothesis is, in some ways, rather difficult to check against the facts. There is always the tempting possibility, when a country experiences, say, a short spurt of growth and then falls back into stagnation, of claiming that true economic development never actually got "under way" in that country. Moreover, there may be "external" factors which complicate the picture. Thus, for example, the Communist Revolution brought a tremendous temporary fall in total Russian production. Does this mean that previous Russian growth was not of the "self-sustaining" type? Or was the fall in production simply a consequence of an "external" interruption to a process that would have continued unabated? The truth is that the "facts" in this area are seldom as clear-cut as we would like to have them.

Second, there are good reasons for believing that self-sustaining elements are not the *only* elements involved in the growth process. As the distinguished American economist, Simon Kuznets, has pointed out, growth may also have certain *self-limiting* features. The old problem of scarce resources and diminishing returns is one such. Others, which Kuznets suggests, are the reduction of economic incentives as incomes rise very high, or the strengthening of vested interests which may resist development in competitive areas of the economy.

Third, it is clear that economic growth is never so automatic and self-reinforcing that a country can't—for example, by unwise economic policies —succeed in getting itself off the track once on it. Argentina would appear to be a case in point. A country which had experienced economic growth in the past and had achieved one of the highest standards of living in Latin America, Argentina, in recent years, has been having great difficulty in sustaining its development effort. Although the figures are open to some question, per-capita income in Argentina appears to have risen less than 14 per cent in total over the whole period from 1950 to 1964; from 1958 to 1964, there appears to have been no increase at all.[9] For a variety of reasons, and in no small measure due to her particular economic policies, Argentina lost what seemed to be a fairly favorable opportunity for continued growth in the post-war period and entered the category of barely developing nations. All this may be temporary, but it does strongly suggest that errors can be made and a growth process halted and even reversed.

Fourth, it is clear that economic growth, however persistent it may be in the long run, is subject to very considerable instability in the short run. The growth process—especially in an unplanned, market economy—is far from smooth. It typically takes place in spurts and thrusts, periods of expanding output and rising prices followed by recessions and contractions in which unemployment and idle capacity cause a slowing down of the rate of advance. In a severe depression—as, for example, in the United States in the 1930's—growth may come to a halt altogether.

This last point refers, of course, to the well-known phenomenon of the *business cycle*. It would take us much too far afield to attempt any kind of analysis of this significant and complicated phenomenon, but it is important for us to notice its existence because it suggests a general point of great interest. The fact is that there may be a considerable difference between the *potential* and the *actual* rate of growth of an economy's output. If, for example, there is increasing unemployment in an economy, then the *actual* expansion of output may be far less than the full-employment *potential* expansion of output. Another way of putting this is to say that for growth to continue it is necessary not only that an economy be *able* to supply an increasing quantity of output but also that there exist proper conditions for *calling forth* that increased supply. Our case of self-sustaining growth was largely confined to the supplying side and therefore suggests a much more continuous pattern of growth than most industrial countries have actually experienced.

When we put these various comments together, they add up to a fairly serious modification of the brave picture of self-generating growth which we drew at the beginning. However, they do not, in the author's opinion, destroy that picture completely. When all is said and done, the hypothesis that modern economic growth tends to be self-sustaining still stands up fairly well under the test of experience. The economies which were growing rapidly in the second half of the nineteenth century or the first half of the twentieth century are, by and large, all still growing rapidly today. The fact that there has been a startling increase in the gap in living standards between those countries which did and those which did not get on the development path during the past century is itself substantial testimony to the fact that modern growth, once begun, tends to maintain itself more often than not.

No one knows, of course, how far into the future this record will ex-

[9] *United Nations Yearbook,* 1965, p. 539.

tend, whether perhaps, at some later or more advanced stage of things, growth will have a tendency to taper off, stop, perhaps even reverse itself. But significantly, this is a question for the future. There is not a single major industrial country in the world at the present moment where a high (by historical standards) rate of economic growth over the next decade is not predicted, expected, and, in fact, demanded. The truth is that most of us who have lived in an industrial economy take continuing economic growth so much for granted that it is actually difficult for us to imagine what life in a stagnant economy would be like.

GETTING STARTED: INDUSTRIAL REVOLUTION, TAKE-OFF, BIG PUSH

The obstacles to development in a poor country and the many elements making for continuing growth in an already developing country largely explain the attention economists have given the problem of "getting started." The degree of attention is indicated by the number of terms used at one time or another to describe the process: *industrial revolution, take-off, big push, initial push, great spurt, breakthrough, critical minimum effort,* and, a few years ago in Communist China, the *great leap forward.* Of course, all these terms have something in common. They all suggest that economic development, instead of beginning slowly and gradually, starts off with a period of intense and concentrated change. Growth begins with a "bang" and not with a "whimper." If a country tries to ease its way into economic development, it may simply remain trapped in the circles of poverty; the initial thrust—so the contention is—must be sufficiently strong to enable the country to take advantage of the cumulative aspects of growth.

This hypothesis rests on the general arguments we have advanced in the last two sections plus the impressionistic historical evidence that growth—at least in its modern form—has made its entry in an essentially "revolutionary" way. If accepted, it is an hypothesis with much relevance to the development problem. For the point of view of the historical study of the growing, industrialized countries, it suggests that one ought to concentrate particular attention on the very early phases of development, attempting to identify the critical changes which were then taking place. Perhaps the most well-known effort to do this in recent years has been that of the economic historian and now Washington advisor W. W. Rostow, who, in an article and later in a best-selling book (*The Stages of Economic Growth*) tried both to define the nature of the *take-off* and to apply the concept to the past experience of the industrial economies of the world.

Rostow's conclusion, as indicated in Table 2-1, was that it was possible to find in the case of each of these countries a period of two or three critical decades in which "both the basic structure of the economy and the social and political structure of the society are transformed in such a way that a steady rate of growth can be, thereafter, regularly sustained." [10] The particular dates given in the table he describes as both "tentative" and "approximate"; but his general contention is evident: The beginnings of growth are looked at in terms of a short period of radical change.

Table 2-1   ROSTOW'S DATING OF VARIOUS TAKE-OFFS

Country	Take-Off	Country	Take-Off
Great Britain	1783-1802	Japan	1878-1900
France	1830-1860	Russia	1890-1914
Belgium	1833-1860	Canada	1896-1914
United States	1843-1860	Argentina	1935-
Germany	1850-1873	Turkey	1937-
Sweden	1878-1900		

These dates represent one economic historian's attempt to locate the critical periods in the development of various countries. Rostow's arguments have excited great interest but also much criticism.

Source: Adapted from Rostow, op. cit., p. 38.

The next question, of course, is: What exactly is it that gets radically changed during these critical short periods? Is there any agreement among economists and historians about what the pivotal changes have been?

In a very broad sense, there is. Thus, there is little doubt that the early stages of growth in the economically advanced countries have regularly witnessed an increase in the rate of technological change. There has similarly been a rise in the percentage of output devoted to capital investment. There have also been important shifts in industrial organization involving an increase in relatively large-scale, more specialized methods of production. In almost all cases, this reorganization has made heavy demands on the labor force and on the entrepreneurial resources of the society.

There is also general agreement that, in the case of the economically advanced countries, there has been some preliminary build-up or "preparation" before these changes occurred. A basic framework of central government has been necessary. There has had to exist a certain nucleus of people devoted to promoting economic progress, whether for personal gain, the welfare of society, military purposes, or whatever. Someone has had to light the spark.

It is when one tries to become more specific than this, however, that the problem (and controversy) begins. Rostow's own attempt to specify the necessary conditions for *take-off* must be regarded as essentially a failure. Thus, for example, he indicated as one of the conditions that savings and investment in an economy must rise from 5 per cent or less to 10 per cent

[10] Rostow, *op. cit.*, pp. 8-9.

or over of the total output of the economy: i.e., that the rate of capital formation doubles during the critical period. Professor Kuznets, dealing with many of the same countries during the same periods, finds that "in no case" does the percentage of capital formation "even approach" a doubling of its value. So far it must be said that these concepts of how a country "gets started" have been more useful in stimulating questions about the historical experience of the economically advanced nations than in giving definite answers.

But they are important questions, as, indeed, are the questions this over-all approach raises with respect to the modern underdeveloped countries. For, if the general view of *take-offs* and *big pushes* is correct, then an underdeveloped country will be likely to achieve development only if it undertakes the effort on a fairly *massive* scale. Such a massive effort may, of course, mean changes in a variety of different areas of the economy at the same time. Or, on the other hand, it may mean a very heavy concentration of effort on some particular "leading sectors" which seem crucial. In either case, the general point remains the same. In order to achieve growth, the underdeveloped country must gird itself for a major assault on its problems.

The implications of such a line of thought are considerable. If, for example, it really is true that an underdeveloped country must begin with a massive development effort, then we must ask: Who will be able to *engineer* such an effort? Can we expect to find in a country which has been buried in poverty for time immemorial a sufficient number of private individuals and entrepreneurs to undertake such a vast program? Or will the state have to step in? And, if the state does step in, what kind of state will it be? Once we admit that development will not automatically occur in these countries and that a decisive effort may have to be made to achieve it, we open a whole range of questions about the methods to be employed which are of enormous political as well as economic significance.

In sum, these notions of how a country "gets started" are relevant both for studying the history of the economically advanced countries and for analyzing the problems currently facing the modern underdeveloped countries. As this point, however, we begin to reach the limits of usefulness of such a completely general approach. The problems of initiating development in the past and in the present show important similarities but *they also show important contrasts*. The Industrial Revolution in late eighteenth-century England may be of the same family as the Chinese dream of a "great leap forward" but it is definitely not the same individual. Even within the group of economically advanced nations, moreover, the process of "getting started" has historically been a very diverse one, depending on such things as when the process began, whether the country was, say, one of the pioneers or was simply following in some other nation's footsteps.

38   To proceed further with the subject, therefore, we must now begin to break it down into less general headings and attempt to understand the forces at work in more particular cases.

SUMMARY

During the past century or two, economists have been trying to find a general theory of the process of economic development. Some have attempted to define various "stages" of development as, for example, through changes in the way exchange is carried out or changes in the importance of different kinds of productive activities. Karl Marx found *his* "stages" in changes in the control of the means of production occurring through the "class struggle." Although Marx's writings have had an enormous impact, particularly in the poorer countries of the world, his failure to foresee the great improvement in living standards in the West or to anticipate the circumstances of later communist revolutions makes him a poor guide when it comes to understanding modern industrial growth.

One early theory that has relevance today is the "classical" theory of development associated with the names of Malthus and Ricardo. These economists concentrated their main attention on two factors—population growth and the limitations on natural resources—and came to the conclusion that the "natural progress" of society was in the direction of a "stationary" state where the population would be living at the "subsistence" level.

The concern about population pressures has brought to the fore modern theories of the "labor surplus" economies. In theory, development occurs in these economies by the transfer of labor from the unproductive (zero marginal product) agricultural sector to the industrial sector at fairly low wages, giving rise to increased industrial production, profits, and reinvestment of earnings. This process works smoothly, however, only when various conditions are fulfilled, including substantial progress in agriculture.

These various theories offer partial insights but not a full-dress analysis of modern development. A more general line of approach involves certain loosely related concepts. These have to do with:

Obstacles to development. Poor countries face very difficult problems in launching modern growth; some economists believe that they suffer from "vicious circles of poverty."

Self-sustaining growth. Growth helps develop the attitudes and mechanisms which will promote further growth. Once established, modern economic growth tends, by and large, to be self-sustaining.

Getting started. Various concepts, such as *take-off, industrial revolution,* and *big push* suggest that the early phases of growth may be critical and that only a fairly substantial change in the structure of the economy may lead a country from chronic poverty to chronic growth.

These various concepts must be qualified in many ways when it comes to specific applications and there is no universal agreement on their proper interpretation. Still, taken together, they do provide us with a point of departure for the study of development problems in a wide variety of contexts.

39

Beginnings of Growth

in the Economically

Advanced Countries

CHAPTER THREE

In this chapter and the next, we shall focus our attention on certain aspects of the development process in the economically advanced countries of the world. In these countries, the launching and sustaining of modern economic growth is already an historical fact. The interesting and sometimes quite different problems facing the modern underdeveloped countries we shall turn to in the concluding section of the book.

GETTING STARTED IN THE PAST

In the present chapter, our particular interest is in the problems of "getting started." How did the process of modern growth in the economically advanced countries begin? Where and when did it first originate? How did it spread from one country to another?

Broadly speaking, the historical beginnings of growth in the **40** developed countries can be said to have had certain common characteristics. There has been:

1. A preliminary period of preparation involving social and political as well as economic change;
2. A rapid increase in the rate of technological progress;
3. Major changes in industrial organization involving: the increased use of capital, the development of larger-scale production units, the adaptation of the labor force to increased mechanization and "division of labor," and a rise of entrepreneurial activity.

In one way or another, all countries which have gone through an industrial revolution have experienced such changes.

Within this broad pattern, however, there have been important variations, depending, in many cases, on whether a country industrialized early or late, whether it was a pioneer or a follower, whether, for example, it originated its own technology or "borrowed" it wholesale from abroad. For this reason it will be useful to divide our discussion into two parts: (1) the first beginnings of modern growth in England; and (2) the somewhat different problems of "getting started" in the countries which followed after.

THE ENGLISH INDUSTRIAL REVOLUTION

The modern economic world can be said to have been born in England in the second half of the eighteenth century.[1] Until that time, economic growth when it had occurred had either been sporadic or very slow; after that time, for England, and subsequently for the countries which followed her lead, rapid growth became a characteristic feature of economic life. It is in this quite definite sense that the English Industrial Revolution marks a new era.

The Long Period of Preparation

The roots of England's great transformation ultimately went far back into past European history. Europe in the Middle Ages was, of course, a rather unlikely spawning-ground for rapid economic progress. It was a poor, overwhelmingly agricultural world; its production was carried out by serf labor on inefficiently organized, largely self-sufficient manorial estates; its feudal lords were more interested in war than economics; its religion deplored the pursuit of gain; there was no effective central government and hardly a semblance of law and order.

[1] The traditional dates given for the English Industrial Revolution are: 1760 to 1832. However, these are not in any way definitive. Rostow, as we have seen, dates the British take-off as occurring in 1783-1802. More recent work suggests that the crucial changes may have come even earlier. Two British economic historians, Phyllis Deane and W. A. Cole, have suggested that the 1740's were a period of great importance. Their book—*British Economic Growth, 1688-1959* (Cambridge: Cambridge University Press, 1962)—gives much useful quantitative material about the British economy in the eighteenth and nineteenth centuries.

Yet even as early as the end of the tenth century an important wedge was beginning to crack this apparently closed circle. There began at that time an expansion of European trade and commerce which one historian has called "probably the greatest turning-point in the history of our civilization." [2] It was all on a very small scale—the cargo of the whole fleet of Venice, the greatest commercial city of the age, would not have filled a single modern freighter—but its effects were profound. The growth of the "extent of the market" tended, wherever it occurred, to undermine the foundations of the feudal and manorial order. Cities and towns began to grow; the new urban markets forced deep changes in an agrarian world which hitherto had been organized by the dictates of local self-sufficiency; small craft industry—even occasional large-scale industry—began to flourish in the wake of the growing commerce. Slow, uneven, reversible as it was, the process of economic change had begun.

These early developments were given an enormous stimulus by a number of interrelated events which began to shape European history significantly from the late fifteenth century on. The discovery of the New World and of new routes to the East further extended European markets and helped cause what amounted to a "commercial revolution." Trade expanded; its focus shifted from the Mediterranean to the Atlantic; colonies were established. In the early sixteenth century, moreover, a flood of gold and silver from the New World began pouring into Spain and thence to the rest of Western Europe. The influx of precious metals was largely responsible for a general rise in prices which not only created favorable economic opportunities but also undercut the traditional social and economic hierarchy. New commercially and financially-minded classes began to rise in the scale of wealth and power.

At the same time, the Renaissance, Reformation, and other cultural currents were working powerful changes in men's attitudes. A secular, materially oriented, intellectually curious society was slowly emerging. In the Middle Ages, the most powerful institution had been the Church; now, increasingly, it was the state. In the Middle Ages, personal profits had been condemned; now "mercantilist" statesmen began to view economic self-interest as a tool for promoting national wealth, power, and prestige. The world of science, tentatively explored in the past, gradually came to include not only a systematic method but a viewpoint which seemed capable of embracing every event in the universe. And all these political, social, and intellectual developments were having direct repercussions in the economic sphere. The new centralized states cleared away local obstacles and helped create national markets for industry and trade. The "Protestant ethic" encouraged industry and thrift, the greatest of virtues for a capital-accumulating society. [3] The

[2] Robert S. Lopez, "The Trade of Medieval Europe: the South," *Cambridge Economic History of Europe*, Vol. II (1952), p. 289.

[3] The relationship of the religious change following the Reformation to subsequent economic developments is both a fascinating and very much debated subject. For

growing enthusiasm for science began to penetrate to untrained laymen who might, on the right occasion, develop some new gadget to increase production or save labor. Slowly still, but perceptibly, the whole structure of the European economy was being re-made.

These several changes were working not only in Europe generally but in England in particular. Indeed, from the sixteenth century onward, they were probably having a more profound effect in England than anywhere on the Continent.

Why England was able to achieve this early lead is, of course, a complex and difficult historical question. She had been able to overcome feudal and urban localism and establish a central government earlier and more effectively than most of the continental countries. Her geographic position was not only a commercial asset but a protection against some of the worst ravages of the wars which periodically devastated the Continent. For a variety of reasons, moreover, England had developed a larger and more vigorous middle class than most of the major European countries. This meant both greater sources of entrepreneurial energy and also a relatively large domestic market which—unlike the luxury market in more aristocratic France—was directed toward "solid conveniences" which could potentially be produced by "mass production" methods.

Whatever the final answers historians may give to the question of England's prominence, it is beyond dispute that, by the eighteenth century, England was exceptionally well-prepared to produce and absorb the changes which the first great breakthrough involved. Three points are crucial:

First, England had already become the acknowledged leader of Europe in science and technology. The scientific "revolution" of the seventeenth century had had an Englishman, Sir Isaac Newton, at its pinnacle. The founding of the Royal Academy in 1600 had been both a symptom and a cause of the general growth of scientific interest. Men in all walks of life—not excluding the English landed aristocracy—were becoming improvement-conscious.

Secondly, England had undergone and was still undergoing a profound reorganization of her agricultural institutions and methods. Under the impact of expanding markets, serfdom had long since disappeared and English landholders had been steadily transforming agriculture into a commercial, surplus-producing operation. Through a process known as *enclosure,* the complicated landholdings of the manorial estates were gradually consolidated, "enclosed" with fences or hedges, placed under individual management, and directed toward market production. The enclosures brought about an extension of the area of productive land in England. Also, by reducing the number of

provocative opinions on this question, the student should read Max Weber's *The Protestant Ethic and the Spirit of Capitalism* (New York: Scribner, 1952), Talcott Parsons (trans.), first published in 1904-1905; and R. H. Tawney, *Religion and the Rise of Capitalism* (New York: Mentor Books, 1952, paperback).

small, inefficient holdings and making possible productive experimentation, they brought a general increase in agricultural production. The increased production served as a base of support for an expansion in the industrial and commercial sectors.[4]

Thirdly and finally, there was England's progress in industry itself. In the sixteenth century England had probably been behind some of the more advanced continental countries; by the eighteenth century she had become the leader. This was true not only in the technology of industry but in its organization as well. In the English brass, copper, iron, and steel industries there were already numerous examples of large-scale undertakings. In the woolen industry, the *merchant-employer,* or "putting out," system had long since been dominant. Under this system the great wool merchants provided the raw materials and goods-in-process and had them "put out" to weavers, spinners, and dyers in the towns and countryside. Unlike the medieval craft shop, these were often very large undertakings, a single merchant employing 500 or even as many as 1,000 persons; they also provided a much clearer division of labor between employer and employee. In general, it can be said that when the great reorganization of English industry began to occur in the late eighteenth century, there was hardly a single feature of the change which had not, at least in some degree, already been anticipated.

When we consider all these points, we can understand why many economic historians feel that the concept of an "industrial revolution," though appropriate elsewhere, is highly misleading in the particular case of England. The length and depth of her earlier preparation, they argue, makes the concept of "evolution" far more appropriate. The counter-argument, of course, is that to use the term "evolution" is to ignore the quantitative significance of changes which produced mankind's first demonstration of rapid and persistent economic growth. Perhaps the best thing to do is to call it a "revolution" but to add quickly that in the case of England—in contrast to some of the countries which followed or are now attempting to follow after—the road to change was exceptionally well-paved.

The Revolution In Technology

The most dramatic of these changes was, without much doubt, the great acceleration of technological progress which occurred in England in the latter part of the eighteenth century. In this respect, the English Industrial Revolution set a universal pattern for the launching of modern economic growth which, at all times and in all places, has involved major innovations in the basic techniques of production. What is more special about the process in

---

[4] England's progress in agriculture prior to and along with her revolution in industry raises an important question about the general nature of the take-off process. Can a country revolutionize her industrial sector without at the same time developing a strong supporting base in agriculture? Or must the two go together? As we shall see in Chapters 5 and 6, this is one of the "key" questions the modern underdeveloped countries must face in their attempts to "get started." (See below, pp. 94-97 and pp. 107-110.)

England was that she was developing this technology largely on her own and in response to already felt economic pressures and needs.

That the changes were startling to those who observed them, contemporary evidence leaves little question. A visiting German found that "the new creations springing into life every year bordered on the fabulous." A Frenchman was startled to find the "night bounded by a circle of fire and the whole country seemed as if lighted by an intense conflagration." An Englishman, and the great innovator in the making of pottery, Josiah Wedgwood, said that the speed of new invention "makes my head giddy. I feel it just as impossible to number the sands of the sea. The difficulties are nearly equal with respect to the cotton trade; with this difference, indeed, that one must shoot here flying, for this darts forward with such an amazing rate as to leave all others far behind."

Table 3-1 SOME INNOVATIONS WHICH USHERED IN THE ENGLISH INDUSTRIAL REVOLUTION

Year	Innovation	Inventors or Innovators	Industry
1709	Coke-smelting process	Abraham Darby	Iron and steel
1733	Flying-shuttle	John Kay	Textiles
1761	Manchester-Worsley Canal	Duke of Bridgewater James Brindley	Water transport
1764	Spinning-jenny	James Hargreaves	Textiles
1769	Steam engine	James Watt	All industry
1769	Water-frame for spinning	Richard Arkwright	Textiles
1776	Introduction of four-course rotation of crops	Coke of Holkham, after the "Norfolk system" of Viscount Townshend	Agriculture
1776	Steam blast for smelting iron with coke	John Wilkinson	Iron and steel
1779	The spinning "mule"	Samuel Crompton	Textiles
1784	Reverberatory furnace with "puddling process"	Henry Cort	Iron and steel
1785	Power loom	Edmund Cartwright	Textiles

This list includes a few of the major innovations which re-shaped British technology and suggests the acceleration of technological progress in the latter half of the eighteenth century.

More prosaic evidence lies in the fact that the number of patents granted for new inventions in the 30 years after 1760 was greater than that of the entire preceding century. Or in a list of some of the actual innovations which were introduced. Table 3-1 is by no means an exhaustive list, and, in many ways, only scratches the surface. There were a whole series of major technological changes in almost every area of the economy: textiles, the basic metallurgical industries, transport, agriculture, animal husbandry, pottery-making. The diversity of areas affected strongly suggests that the revolution in technology was not the product of any single set of inventions—even of

45

such an important innovation as the introduction of steam power. It was much more the product of a growing awareness of the general possibilities of technological change. The search for, and the expectation of finding, improved methods of production was being imbedded in the fundamental attitudes of the society.

This search, in turn, was in the case of England very much conditioned by the pattern of economic pressures which were developing simultaneously with the new technology. The inventors and innovators were not speculating at random. With the partial exception of James Watt, who was better trained and more systematically scientific than most of them, they were practical men of affairs who were engaged in finding solutions to concrete problems and bottlenecks. Sometimes the problem was a scarcity of resources, as in the case of the shortage of timber and charcoal in the later eighteenth century, which led, among other things, to the invention of the "puddling process" by which coal could be substituted for charcoal in the refining of malleable iron. Sometimes it was pressure produced by the needs of other industries. Thus, much of the progress in canal construction can be regarded as a response to the need for finding a cheap means of transporting coal.

Sometimes the bottlenecks derived from within the industry itself. Technological progress in one stage of the productive process would set up pressure for improvements in those which were lagging behind. The classic example of this particular pattern of change was in the cotton textile industry, the most spectacularly growing industry of the English Industrial Revolution. Progress in one branch of the industry (weaving) created needs which were met by progress in another branch (spinning), which, in turn, created pressures on the first branch in a continuing process of technological change.[5]

The significance of these various examples is this: The progress of English technology in this period, as dramatic as it was, proceeded in an essentially step-by-step fashion in a pattern dictated by the prevailing needs and conditions of the country's economy. The *kind* of technology which evolved was one well-suited both to the natural resources and other factors of production available to England and also to the immediately preceding state of technology out of which it grew. This point is of some importance. When we compare England to some of the countries which industrialized later, we can see that it was a great disadvantage for her to have to develop her own technological revolution rather than to be able to borrow it ready-made from

[5] Thus, John Kay's flying-shuttle in the early eighteenth century greatly speeded up the weaving process which increased the demand for yarn and thus the need for improvements in spinning. The pressure became so intense that in 1760 the Society for the Encouragement of the Arts, Manufactures, and Commerce began offering prizes for a new spinning machine. The result was James Hargreaves' spinning-jenny. The spinning process was further improved in the following years by the development of the water-frame and of Samuel Crompton's spinning "mule." But now the weavers were lagging behind. As a consequence, beginning in 1785 with Cartwright's rather imperfect power loom, the long and fateful process of the application of steam power in the weaving industry got underway.

someone else. In this *particular* respect, however, she had a certain advantage. Because the new technology was developed internally on her own home grounds, it came at a pace and in a shape peculiarly appropriate to her own productive needs.

The Factory System

England's take-off into modern growth involved not only an accelerated pace of technological advance but also a basic reorganization of the industrial structure, most dramatically in the beginnings of the *factory system*. The new machinery made larger-scale units desirable. Larger-scale units facilitated the use of the new machinery. The *factory,* not completely unknown to Britain in the past, made its first major appearance on the world's industrial scene.

What, exactly, is a *factory?* Many definitions have been offered at one time or another but the central elements are fairly clear: (1) The new factories involved a greater use of capital and machinery and an expanded scale of production as compared with previous industrial units. (2) They involved, in contrast to the merchant-employer system, the centralization of production in a single shop or building. (3) They brought about a much greater "division of labor" and a still wider gap between employer and employee. (4) They required a new "discipline" in the labor force, a reflection of the fact that the tempo of work was no longer set by the mood or habit of the individual workmen but by a synchronized production process and, more particularly, by the rhythms of the machine.

The factory, then, can be looked on as a form of industrial organization in which many of the key factors in economic development—increased scale, specialization, added capital per worker, and improved technology—were united to produce massive increases in total and per capita output.

But how were these factories introduced? The transformation to the new system required the mobilization of funds which could be used to secure the machinery and other capital which the larger and more mechanized units demanded. It required additional labor; labor, moreover, which would submit to the new industrial discipline. It required, furthermore, a group of men who had the economic foresight not only to understand the new opportunities but also to devise ways of bringing the labor, capital, and technology together in a functioning operation. There were, in short, heavy demands not only on the factors of production but on the more intangible factor of *entrepreneurship* as well.

One of the striking things about the English Industrial Revolution is that these demands were met almost exclusively by private individuals, without any substantial foreign assistance and with a minimum of interference (help or hindrance) from the state. The age of the first modern breakthrough was also in large measure an age of *laissez faire*.

In order to understand this fact, we must recall the special features of **47** the British situation. In the first place, the long prior expansion of the

British economy meant that she was above the "subsistence" level when the Industrial Revolution occurred. There were important sources of capital in commerce, agriculture, and industry which private individuals could draw on from the very beginning.

In the second place, because it was a step-by-step process, the English Industrial Revolution was typically geared to what was privately achievable and not to a sudden "re-making" of the whole order of society. In point of fact, the actual introduction of the factory system in England was, by modern standards, a rather slow, drawn-out process. In 1830, for example, there were still four times as many hand looms as power looms in England, and this despite the fact that it was the textile industry which was the exemplar of British progress. Indeed, it has been estimated that in the mid-nineteenth century, the large-scale, mechanized industries which had already made Britain the "workshop of the world" employed only 1.7 million workers out of a total population of 21 million. This is not to deny the importance of the new factories—in a way, it simply proves how enormously efficient they were! —but simply to suggest that the transformation of the English economy proceeded at a reasonably manageable pace.

Finally, because the changes involved no sharp discontinuities, it was generally possible for individuals to start on a comparatively small scale and then to expand by reinvesting their profits. Josiah Wedgwood grew rich this way, beginning with virtually nothing and leaving at his death a personal estate of £245,000. Richard Arkwright, who actually began as a wigmaker, left double that sum, having earlier bragged that if he could only live long enough he would have sufficient money to pay back the national debt. The habit of reinvesting of profits seems to have been strong from the very beginning. T. S. Ashton, one of the world's leading authorities on the English Industrial Revolution, cites the case of Samuel Walker and Co.:

> Year after year some addition, great or small, was made to the plant. . . . It was not, apparently, until 1757, when the stock had reached £7,500, that the Walkers allowed themselves a dividend—of £140; and throughout, the proportion of the profit that was distributed remained small. Thus it came about that by 1774 the capital had reached £62,500 . . . Whatever may be said against the early employers, the charge of self-indulgence can hardly be laid at their door.[6]

Thus, small beginnings were possible and the prevalent attitudes—a product of the long prior social and economic evolution—were favorable to making the most of the opportunities offered. Under such circumstances, private individuals could and did secure their own capital resources as they went along.

The fact that the first industrial revolution in the world's history took

[6] T. S. Ashton, *The Industrial Revolution* (London: Home University Library of Modern Knowledge, 1948), pp. 86-87.

place in a privately oriented, essentially *laissez-faire* environment is one of considerable significance. It has had a profound influence on both economic theory and practice in England, the United States, and many other countries of the world. Until quite recently, indeed, the study of economic growth and the study of the rise of private "capitalism" were often treated as virtually synonymous.

Because of this identification, it is all the more important that we recognize that the English experience, in this respect, has not in fact been universal. The long preparation and the relatively gradual nature of the technological and industrial changes confronted English entrepreneurs with a task which, though difficult, was essentially manageable. Under such circumstances, *laissez faire* may easily have been—as Adam Smith, David Ricardo, and most other contemporary British economists believed it to be—the most effective course of action. In later situations, however, the task facing private entrepreneurs has sometimes turned out to be rather different from what it was in the late eighteenth-century England. And, in these situations, as history has shown, countries have not hesitated to depart very considerably from the English example.

England's Achievement

A history of slow advance and preparation, a marked acceleration of the rate of technological progress, the beginnings of the factory system—these were the ingredients of the English Industrial Revolution. What, then, were its consequences?

Certainly not all of them were pleasant. The new machinery and industrial organization benefited certain groups in society, but it hurt others and, in general, it gave a profound wrench to the entire social order. For the child of five whose job it was to work all day picking up bits of cotton waste from around the machinery in the new textile factories it was not clear that economic "progress" was the answer to his prayers. One need not glorify previous social and economic conditions to realize that the English Industrial Revolution produced a collection of horror stories peculiarly its own.

From the point of view of economic development, however, our particular interest is in the growth of British production which the Industrial Revolution made possible. As a consequence of the technological and industrial changes, certain industries, like cotton textiles, shot forward at a pace never before conceived possible. Other industries followed along in the general advance. In 40 years, coal output increased 10 times. In 1788 pig-iron production was 68,000 tons; in 1839 it was 1,347,000 tons. Moreover, and most significantly of all, this general expansion of production did not halt in the early nineteenth century with the "closing" of the period of the Revolution proper; it continued during the ensuing century and a half at rates which, though varying, were persistently higher than anything known prior to the eighteenth century.

49

Table 3-2 GREAT BRITAIN'S IMPORTS OF RAW COTTON
IN SELECTED YEARS

Year	Weight of Raw Cotton Imported (in millions of pounds)	Year	Weight of Raw Cotton Imported (in millions of pounds)
1701	1	1784	11.5
1751	3	1789	32.6
1771	4.8	1799	43
1781	5.3	1802	60.5

The rapidity of progress in the British cotton textile industry is suggested by these rough figures on the imports of raw cotton. In 1781-1802 alone, they increased elevenfold.

Source: Paul Mantoux, *Industrial Revolution in the Eighteenth Century,* 2nd ed. (New York: Harcourt, Brace, 1927.)

Figure 3-1, taken from the indices prepared by Professor Walther Hoffman, gives the broad sweep of the advance in British industrial production from the Industrial Revolution to 1950.

Since the measurement of economic growth over long periods involves some difficult problems, the following general points should be kept in mind:

FIG. 3-1 Total industrial production (including building) in the British Economy, 1760-1950, selected years (1913 = 100). (Source: Walter G. Hoffman, *British Industry 1700-1950,* Oxford: Basil Blackwell, 1955, Table 54.)

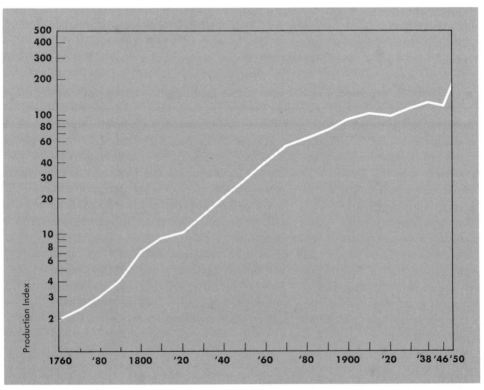

1. The statistics for earlier historical periods are almost always inadequate and fragmentary. The gathering of statistics is one of the later by-products of economic development.
2. All measurements of long-run growth involve serious conceptual difficulties. The structure of production in the economy is constantly changing; new products are being introduced. These problems pose a difficult challenge to the ingenuity (and conscience) of the statistician.
3. Many important aspects of the growth process are not covered in the usual figures and diagrams on growth. Increases in "leisure" are not included. Conversely, there are productive "costs" involved in industrialization, but these are not deducted.

In view of these and other problems, all measurements of long-run economic growth must be taken as approximations only.

So much for difficulties. As to basic significance, the picture presented fairly well tells the story. According to Hoffman's estimates, total British industrial output increased *by more than 70 times* over the 190 years from 1760 to 1950. In the next chapter, when we consider the economic development of the United States, we shall not find such figures so startling. But by any previous historical standard, they are little short of miraculous. As a consequence of her Industrial Revolution, England gave the world the first clear-cut example of the modern style of economic growth. She had accomplished the breakthrough.

BEGINNINGS OF MODERN DEVELOPMENT
IN OTHER COUNTRIES

Ever since the English Industrial Revolution, social critics have spoken of the costs of industrialization and the harmful effects of mechanization and standardization in dehumanizing our lives. Value judgments aside, however, the process of industrialization has had a seemingly irresistible forward momentum. When nations have had a meaningful opportunity to choose, they have invariably elected the path of economic development despite the social costs involved.

The Spread of Industrialization

Such was the case in the period following England's achievement of industrial supremacy. One by one, other countries have risen up to challenge and, in some cases, to surpass her. As these other countries have achieved development, Britain's relative position has naturally declined. As late as 1870, the United Kingdom produced 31.8 per cent of the entire world's manufacturing output; by the 1920's her share had fallen to less than 10 per cent. The outstanding challengers during this period were Germany and particularly the United States. Thus, for example, during the 20 years between 1893 and 1913, while Britain's steel production was increasing by a healthy

136 per cent, Germany's was increasing by a remarkable 522 per cent and that of the United States by a miraculous 715 per cent. In the twentieth century, indeed, it has been the United States which has enjoyed the economic predominance which England had a century earlier. And, as the recent surges of Russia, Continental Europe, and Japan suggest, we, too, are to have our challengers in the years ahead.

Where did modern industrialism take root in the world? Not everywhere, as we know. The majority of the world's population was affected little, or not at all (or perhaps even adversely), by these revolutionary changes. For the most part, the countries which succeeded in achieving modern development after England were either in Europe or in areas of European settlement such as the United States, Canada, Australia, and New Zealand. The common cultural background meant that many of the key attitudes and institutions which had been important in the English case were also present in these other areas to at least some degree from the very beginning. From a more physical point of view, the countries were all located in the temperate zone; and in many cases, particularly in the newly settled areas, there was an abundance of land and other natural resources in relation to population. Until very recently, then, modern development produced its main effects in countries which were closely linked with Europe and England in particular, and where natural circumstances were generally favorable.

There are, however, some exceptions to this general rule and it is important to keep these in mind. Perhaps the best single illustration is the case of Japan. Japan in the late nineteenth century not only suffered from a high ratio of population to land but also was a country with a non-Western culture which, until the coming of Commodore Perry in 1853, had been almost completely isolated from the outside world. Nevertheless, following the restoration of the emperor in 1868, Japan deliberately set out to achieve the kind of rapid economic development she had observed in the West. The results were impressive: Railroad mileage increased from virtually nothing in 1870 to 3,855 miles in 1900; pig-iron production increased sevenfold from 1874 to 1900; in the same period mineral production increased over 20 times and rice output rose from 119.1 million bushels (1873) to 205.6 million bushels (1900). Because she started at a much lower level than most other economically developed countries and also because of such other problems as population pressures and disastrous wars, Japan's standard of living today is well below that of most Western developed countries. Nevertheless, her strong beginning, plus her very rapid rate of growth in the last two decades, makes it clear that she has mastered the secret of sustained economic growth. Her example definitely suggests that the modern industrial engine can be introduced under a wide variety of conditions.[7]

[7] For a good general account of early Japanese economic progress, see W. W. Lockwood, *The Economic Development of Japan: Growth and Structural Change, 1869-1938* (Princeton: Princeton University Press, 1954).

Some Characteristics of Later Beginnings

The problems of "getting started" in these various countries were, of course, very diverse, depending on particular historical, cultural, and physical circumstances. As in the case of England, there were certain general preparatory changes followed by the rapid introduction of new technology and of larger-scale, more capital-intensive industries. But conditions differed from country to country and, more to the point, they differed substantially from those which had faced England by virtue of the fact that England had already broken the ground. In one degree or another, these later beginnings are all characterized by their having taken place in a world where an industrial revolution had occurred and where continued economic and technological progress was a fact of life. Thus, when we compare them with England's, we find some important contrasts of a fairly general nature.

1. The existence of an England which had already made great strides toward industrialization served as an important stimulus to these countries in terms of technology, capital, and example. It was no longer necessary to invent the steam engine. The whole range of English technological achievements could be copied and applied, with modifications, in the new contexts. Not only this, but British technicians and British capital were often available to put the improved technology into effect. British private foreign investment grew to enormous proportions particularly in the half century or so before the First World War. In the 1880's and again in 1911-1913, as much as 6.5 per cent of British national income was going into new foreign investments. Finally, and in some ways most significant of all, was the simple fact that England had created a model and a target. She had given all these countries the *concept* of an "industrial revolution."

In general, then, we can say that England's earlier achievements substantially affected both the goals and means of subsequent efforts to industrialize. This does not mean that the *strains* of these efforts were always less; in some cases they were probably greater. After the English Industrial Revolution, countries like Japan and Russia, with relatively little prior preparation, could now attempt to revolutionize their economies overnight; the wrench in the established social, political, and economic system was often a profound one.

2. The continuing evolution of technology over the decades meant a change in the nature of the industries which began to surge ahead in the take-off period. In the case of England, cotton textiles had led the way. In the countries which followed after, although the textile industry continued to be important, we often find other industries, and particularly the railroads, playing a dominant role in the early stages of industrialization. The railroads were crucial because they made possible the unification of large market areas and brought cost reductions to virtually every particular industry in the economy. They were almost certainly the "key" industry in the case of the

53

United States, but they were hardly less significant for Europe. The expansion of European railway mileage from 1,930 miles in 1840 to 32,240 miles in 1860, and then again to 104,580 miles in 1880, involved a kind of effort and produced an economic result whose magnitude is difficult to exaggerate.

The fact that subsequent breakthroughs were typically linked to the expansion of the railroads meant that the amount of real investment required in these countries often exceeded what it had been in England. Railroad construction typically involves a very heavy capital outlay; it became more difficult for private individuals to secure the necessary capital without recourse to foreign assistance, the banking system, or the state.

3. Finally, and partly for the above reasons, the state typically played a larger role in the initiation of industrial development in these countries than it had in England. This generalization is, of course, fraught with difficulties. There were many countries, like the United States, where, despite the intervention of government (state and local as well as federal), the *central* vehicle for initiating growth was clearly private initiative and entrepreneurship. Moreover, it is probably true in *all* of these countries that the beginnings of modern development were accompanied by a rise of individual energy and enterprise as against the traditional social restraints.

Nevertheless, when we look at the major countries of Continental Europe, and at Russia and Japan, the generally increased role of the state becomes evident. The Japanese case is, again, a very interesting one. Japan not only attempted to modernize under extremely difficult conditions but also attempted to do so with only limited assistance from foreign capital. Given the special difficulties of her circumstances it seems doubtful whether completely unassisted private parties would have been up to the task of getting this extremely "backward" country on the road to development. In point of fact, the Japanese state, led by an energetic group of samurai-bureaucrats in the period following the restoration of the emperor in 1868, took a very active role both directly, as the entrepreneur in initiating various industries, and, indirectly, by a variety of measures to encourage and direct private investment, in accomplishing the initial thrust.[8]

More generally, these departures from the *laissez-faire* approach seem to have reflected: (a) the linking of economic and political objectives, economic development being seen as the road to national and international political power; (b) the desire, in the face of the success of England and other previous developers, to push forward more rapidly than a "gradualistic" approach might allow; and (c) the increased difficulty, as we have already mentioned, of securing the necessary capital through private channels when

---

[8] Direct state intervention in Japan in the early stages of growth frequently took the form of governmental initiative in establishing new enterprises which were then subsequently turned over to large private capitalistic concerns. Thus, direct public ownership may actually have been on the decline in Japan from the late nineteenth century until the 1930's. In general, government and business worked together in a close relationship throughout Japan's modern history.

faced with the heavy demand of such capital-intensive industries as the railroads.

For all these reasons, although economic development in the "late-comers" has typically witnessed a surge of individualism as against the old hierarchic social order, it has also witnessed, at least in its initial stages, a substantial increase in the activities of the state.

The Russian Case

The most dramatic example of such state intervention has, of course, occurred in Russia. Because of its great international importance, Russia's performance requires at least a mention.

Very briefly, Russia presents many of the most striking characteristics of the "late-comer." As late as 1928, the Soviet Union with a population four times greater than that of Great Britain produced a total industrial output of only one-quarter of Britain's: a ratio in per-capita terms of 1 to 16! During Russia's earlier history, this economic backwardness was manifested in institutions and practices which, by West European standards, were sharply anachronistic. In England, for example, serfdom had disappeared for all practical purposes by the middle of the sixteenth century. In Russia, two centuries later, roughly 15 million out of the country's 19 million people were serfs. Even industrial enterprises often used serf labor. It was not until 1861, a hundred years after England began her breakthrough, that the Russian serfs were finally emancipated.

The fact that Russia has always been behind, that she has had so far to go to "catch up," and that the initiation of economic changes has been plagued by difficult social and institutional obstacles—all these have un-doubtedly had a bearing on the mechanism by which Russian industrializa-tion has been achieved. The great role played by the state in the twentieth-century Soviet Union is not, in fact, a complete novelty in Russian experience. When Russia made her first early industrial advance under Peter the Great (1682-1725), it was government initiative, particularly for the purpose of strengthening the army and navy, which was decisive. Peter's visits to England and Western Europe and his hiring of foreign technicians are well known; but he also used the state treasury directly to initiate the building of factories and new industries, and, in general, employed his powers as absolute monarch to push Russia forward at as fast a pace as possible.

Russia remained in a position of relative backwardness, however, and it was not until the late nineteenth and early twentieth centuries that a "big push" was seriously attempted. Here, again, state entrepreneurship was of vital importance. The Czarist government financed much of Russia's railroad construction; the state bank lent assistance to private enterprises; the govern-ment continued to press for the entry of technicians and technology from abroad; government tariffs were used to protect new industries; moreover, by heavy taxation of the peasantry, the state managed indirectly to cause

55

the export of large quantities of grain and thus to achieve a favorable balance of trade and the funds to secure foreign loans which could then be used for developmental purposes. State initiative was, of course, not the only factor in Russia's attempt to "get started" during this period, but it was an important one and certainly far more significant than it had ever been in the case of England.

Whether this particular approach would have been sufficient to launch Russia permanently on the path of modern development, we shall never know conclusively. World War I, the Revolution, and a drastic reorganization of Russian political, social, and economic life intervened. When Russia resumed her forward progress in the late twenties it was, as we know, under a rigidly planned and state-dominated regime. This regime has been deeply influenced by what one expert has called an "obsession with the need for rapid growth." [9] By means which were often coercive and through an emphasis on high investment, low consumption, industrial development at the expense of agriculture, and increased scientific and technical education, the Soviet state has forced a rate of growth that has brought her an industrial output that today exceeds any country in Europe and is second to the United States. [10]

This performance, apart from its obvious political implications, is significant for the student of economic development in several ways. In the first place, it proves more or less conclusively that an industrial revolution of major proportions can be accomplished under even the most rigidly state-dominated system. However much we may dislike the methods, the results are clear, impressive, and really unarguable.

In the second place, the Russian record suggests some of the weaknesses of such an approach to the development problem. Russia has achieved enormous progress in industry but her progress in agriculture and in the area of consumer goods generally has lagged far behind. Partly, of course, this has been a matter of explicit policy. Consumption competes with investment and growth; agriculture with modern heavy industry. But it has not been completely a matter of choice. The fact is that the stark methods of planning and control which produce clear results in industry seem to work notably *less* well in the agricultural sphere. Indeed, in recent years, there has been a growing awareness among Soviet economists and even Soviet officials of a general need for increasing the efficiency of the economy by allowing at least some play for market forces. In the early 1960's, reforms in this direction were urged by a Soviet economist by the name of E. G. Liberman and, in 1965, a modified form of "Libermanism" was applied to all industrial enterprises. It is not yet clear how far the Russian leadership will carry these reforms and,

[9] Robert W. Campbell, *Soviet Economic Power,* 2nd ed. (Cambridge: Houghton Mifflin, 1966), p. 26.

[10] Gross national product in the USSR is, however, still substantially behind that of the United States, particularly in the consumption-goods category. In other categories, however, and especially those having to do with military strength or industrial investment, the efforts of the two countries are much more comparable.

at the moment, they do not appear to have made basic inroads on the Soviet system. However, the weaknesses of the Russian economy which have called forth this re-evaluation should serve as a warning for any country wishing to model itself on the Soviet system, particularly, it may be added, if the country is one in which increased agricultural production has high priority.

Finally, the Russian experience contains a kind of warning for us also. Professor Alexander Gerschenkron puts the matter this way:

> The Soviet government can be properly described as a product of the country's economic backwardness. . . . If anything is a "grounded historical assumption," this would seem to be one: the delayed industrial revolution was responsible for a political revolution in the course of which the power fell in the hands of a dictatorial government . . . It is not only Russia but the whole world that pays the price for the failure to emancipate the Russian peasants and to embark upon industrialization policies at an early time. Advanced countries cannot afford to ignore economic backwardness.[11]

At a time when over half the world's population lives in a condition of economic "backwardness" far exceeding even that of pre-Revolutionary Russia, this is clearly an important moral to keep in mind.

SUMMARY

In this chapter we have discussed the problem of "getting started" in the economically advanced countries of the world.

The English Industrial Revolution. The English Industrial Revolution, beginning in the latter part of the eighteenth century, marks the first real breakthrough into modern growth. In the case of England, the forces which produced this breakthrough had been building up slowly over the course of many centuries so that the event, when it came, found a context already well-prepared.

The most significant aspects of the period were a marked acceleration of technological progress and the beginnings of the modern factory system. Through a succession of new techniques and innovations, the basic technology of production was subject to continuous changes in many different areas of the economy. This new technology, in turn, gradually became embodied in larger-scale, centralized factories requiring a greater use of capital and a disciplined labor force.

As dramatic as these changes were, they were nevertheless carried out in an essentially step-by-step way and in a shape determined by the country's prevailing economic conditions. This fact helps explain, among other things,

---

[11] Alexander Gerschenkron, "Economic Backwardness in Historical Perspective," in Bert F. Hosetitz (ed.), *The Progress of Underdeveloped Areas* (Chicago: University of Chicago Press, 1952), pp. 27-29.

how private British entrepreneurs were able to take the initiative for this major transformation of the society without any substantial foreign assistance and under an essentially *laissez-faire* regime.

The Industrial Revolution necessarily involved social costs. From the point of view of growth, however, the results are clear: The British economy saw the beginning of a general, long-run expansion of output more rapid than anything the world had ever witnessed before.

Beginnings of modern development in other countries. Other countries followed after Britain's lead, some, like the United States, soon surpassing her. In general, the growth process took root in Europe and in countries linked with Europe, and in favorable geographic circumstances. But there were exceptions, as in the case of Japan.

Generally speaking, the process of "getting started" in the countries which followed after differed from that of England in these respects: (1) The existence of an industrialized England made available to these countries an already invented technology, important assistance in the form of British foreign investment, and, not least, the simple example of British achievements. (2) The continuing evolution of technology meant that new industries, notably the railroads, often played a vital role in these later take-offs. (3) The state— partly for political objectives, partly because of the desire to "catch up" rapidly, and partly because of the demands of more capital-intensive in- dustries—typically played a larger role in initiating development in the "late- comers" than it had in England.

In this last respect, Russia is, of course, the most clear-cut example. Despite definite areas of weakness in her approach, Russia has demonstrated that it is possible to initiate rapid modern growth even under a rigidly state- dominated regime, a fact of great significance, politically as well as economi- cally, in the modern world.

The Growth

of the American Economy

Our discussion of the economically advanced countries in the last chapter was largely confined to the problems of "getting started"; now it is time to consider some of the implications of sustained, long-run growth. We shall concern ourselves here with only one country, the United States. Partly, this is a matter of space; partly it is because the United States, more than any other nation in the world, demonstrates the extraordinary impact of the forces of modern industrial change. At the present time, the American economy produces as much total output as the bottom 60 per cent or 70 per cent of the world's population. Although she started later than England, her level of output per capita is now at least twice that of the former mother country. Even Russia, despite her rapid post-war growth, produces no more than half as much total output as the United States, and this with a larger population. It is in the United States, then, that we can best understand the full scope and potentialities of modern development.

THE FAVORABLE BACKGROUND
OF AMERICAN GROWTH

In attempting to assess the economic achievements of the United States, we should, of course, remember that they were accomplished under exceptionally favorable conditions. These were **59** not only, and probably not even primarily, geographic conditions;

there were favorable political, social, cultural, and historical conditions as well.

The United States, for example, has enjoyed a rare degree of political stability. Except for the Civil War, there was not a single conflict on American soil during the whole period of its industrial development. In a deeper sense, the American form of government has proved to be both eminently durable and yet also flexible as the occasion required. Individuals have been able to go about their business in an orderly community with the basic assurance that they would be able to enjoy the fruits of their own labors; at the same time, the rule of order has never been dogmatic and authoritarian but practical and democratic, adjusting itself to new situations and to the needs of the people.

Then there was the cultural and historical heritage of the American people. The United States derived its being from Europe and from England in particular and, as such, was immediate heir to all the accumulated knowledge and skills which had been built up over the course of the centuries in the Old World. This accumulation was further enriched by the steady stream of immigrants which flowed to American shores during the country's development, bringing skills, talents, flexibility, and a general diversification of the sources upon which economic progress could draw.

The United States not only inherited much from Europe but did so in a context of the wide open spaces, rich in natural resources, and without the encumbrance of the traditions and old feudal relics with which many parts of Europe were still struggling even in the nineteenth century. One of the most striking things about the American people from the very beginning has been their mobility. The country, literally, has always been on the move: from East to West, from farm to factory, from country to city. But, equally significant, has been the degree of social and economic mobility. The absence of a feudal past, the existence of a "frontier," and the prevalence of a social and political theory which emphasized equal rights for all citizens— all these conspired to create unparalleled opportunities for individuals to better their status. "Rags to riches" is partly myth; but it has also been part of the American reality. It is one of the reasons, among others, why the Marxian concept of "class struggle" has had so little relevance to the American scene.

All this is not meant to suggest that conditions in the United States were always, and in each and every respect, favorable to economic development. There was, for example, the institution of slavery which, apart from its moral implications, was ultimately incompatible with an industrial civilization. Nor should we forget that much of American economic development took place with a highly inadequate banking, monetary, and fiscal system; indeed, crisis and instability were often the order of the day. The "panics" of 1819, 1837, 1857, 1873, 1893, 1907, and 1914, not to mention the sharp contraction of business activity in 1920-1921 and the massive Depression which began in 1929 and lasted through the whole decade of the thirties—all these events suggest that American institutions were by no means attuned to the requirements of orderly economic growth.

Still, in any over-all view of American history, it is clear that the favorable circumstances have far and away dominated the unfavorable. Indeed, it is doubtful whether quite such opportune conditions for achieving economic development have occurred in any other country of the world, before or since.

MAJOR TRENDS IN AMERICAN ECONOMIC DEVELOPMENT

In order to understand what continuing modern growth has meant to the American economy, let us summarize a few of the main economic trends in the United States over the past century or more.

In the year 1800 America was still a small, agrarian country. Its population was a little over 5 million people, its territory limited to the present Northeast and South. Roughly 80 per cent of the labor force was engaged in agriculture. The new nation exported raw materials and processed foodstuffs and imported manufactures from abroad. Despite its smaller population, the United States had as many farmers as England, but when it came to manufacturing and trade, England's labor force outnumbered the American by 14 to 1. Given the favorable natural conditions, living standards in the young country were tolerable, but in terms of the degree of industrialization and, more generally, in terms of economic potential, the United States was clearly an "underdeveloped" country.

How this situation changed in the course of American development can be shown by a variety of different measures.

Growth In Population

Perhaps the first dramatic change to catch the eye is the enormous increase in the American population, amounting to over 30 times during the period 1800-1960. This great increase in population was partly fed by immigration and partly by natural increase. Interestingly enough, as important as immigration has been in American history, it actually explains well under half of the total increase in population during this period, the more important factor being the excess of births over deaths.[1] As we would

[1] At its height, in the late nineteenth and early twentieth century, net immigration into the United States varied between a quarter and a third of the country's over-all population increase. Simple fractions, of course, do not tell the full story of the impact of immigration on the economic development of the United States. Thus, for example, the fact that there were more male immigrants than female and that they were more highly concentrated in the productive (as opposed to dependent) age groups meant that they had a very strong effect on the American labor force. Since immigration tended to vary according to business conditions in the United States, moreover, the country had a cushion against labor shortages which might develop in times of prosperity.

61

expect, there has been a persistent fall in the American death-rate owing both to improved economic conditions and to progress in public health and medical care. Table 4-1 shows one of the more significant aspects of American economic and scientific progress over the past century: an increase in life expectancy of over 30 years, or roughly 75 per cent.

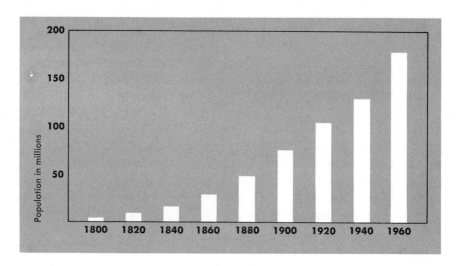

FIG. 4-1 United States' Population: 1800-1960. (Source: Elizabeth W. Gilboy and Edgar M. Hoover, "Population and Immigration," in Seymour Harris [ed.], *American Economic History*, New York: McGraw-Hill, 1961; U.S. Bureau of the Census.)

As far as the birth-rate is concerned, it was very high in the early 1800's, but was on the decline for the remainder of the century. Beginning long before the Civil War and continuing until the end of the nineteenth century, there was a trend in America both toward later marriages and smaller families. This trend, similar to trends in most other developing countries, has often been attributed to the direct or indirect effects of the industrialization process.[2] In recent decades, the birth-rate in the United States has varied considerably. From a low of about 18 per thousand in the Depression of the thirties, it

[2] There are several reasons why economic development might tend to lower a country's birth-rate. Here are a few which are sometimes offered: (1) Urban living is less conducive to child-rearing than rural living. (2) Industrial development means that women have job and career opportunities which they may prefer to their traditional roles as mothers and home-makers. (3) A rising standard of living may make parents want educational and other advantages for their children which can be better secured with smaller families. (4) Furthermore, the very fact that economic development tends to bring lower infant mortality rates means that parents need have fewer children to achieve a family of any given size. In general, it can be said that birth-rates in economically advanced countries tend to be considerably lower than those of poor, underdeveloped countries.

Table 4-1 INCREASING LIFE EXPECTANCY IN THE UNITED STATES

Year	Average of Male and Female Life Expectancies at Birth, Years *
1850	39.4
1878-1882	42.6
1890	43.5
1900-1902	49.24
1909-1911	51.49
1919-1921	56.40
1929-1931	59.20
1939-1941	63.62
1949-1951	68.07
1954	69.6
1963	69.6

* For years 1850, 1878-1882, and 1890, life expectancies are for Massachusetts only.

An important aspect of the development of the United States as of other industrial countries has been the dramatic increase in life expectancies recorded over the past century.

Source: Gilboy and Hoover, op. cit.; Statistical Abstract of the U.S., 1965.

rose to about 25 per thousand in the early post-war period. Since the late 1950's, it has been once again on the decline, being estimated at 19.4 per thousand in 1965. This present U.S. birth-rate is very low compared to most underdeveloped countries. However, as all present-day students know, the temporary increase in the American birth-rate in the late 1940's and early 1950's has brought great pressure on our schools and colleges in the 1960's.

Changes in Where, at What, and How Much We Work

Americans not only live longer now than they did at the beginning of the nineteenth century, they also live in different places, work at different occupations, and enjoy more leisure time.

In the year 1800 the United States was an overwhelmingly rural country; at present, nearly two-thirds of its population lives in urban areas. In the

Table 4-2 URBANIZATION IN THE UNITED STATES

Year	Percentage of Population in Urban Areas	Year	Percentage of Population in Urban Areas
1800	5.6	1900	39.7
1820	7.3	1920	51.3
1840	10.5	1930	56.2
1860	19.7	1940	56.5
1880	28.1	1950	59.0

Economic development and increasing urbanization typically go together.

Source: Peter B. Kenen, "Statistical Survey of Basic Trends," in Harris (ed.), American Economic History, op. cit.

United States, as in every economically advanced country, development and urbanization have gone hand in hand.

This shift from country to town, of course, has been largely a reflection of profound shifts in the structure of the occupations in which Americans have been engaged. If, as some would argue, the clearest sign of economic development is a decline in the percentage of the labor force in agriculture, then there can be little doubt of the pace of American development. From the community of 1800 with its 80 per cent of the labor force in agriculture, the United States has shown a continually declining percentage over time until, at present, it is 10 per cent or less. Moreover, the percentage is still dropping and the presence of substantial unutilized productive capacity on our farms is easy proof of the fact that this revolutionary transformation was not accompanied by empty stomachs and austerity.

Table 4-3 PERCENTAGE DISTRIBUTION OF EMPLOYMENT OF THE U.S. LABOR FORCE *

Year	Agriculture, Fishing & Forestry	Mining	Manufacture, Construction †	Transport, Communications, Commerce & Finance	Professions, Government, Other Services ‡
1820	72.0	—	—	—	—
1860	59.9	1.6	18.5	7.5	12.5
1870	50.8	1.6	23.5	11.5	12.8
1880	50.5	1.8	23.2	12.1	12.2
1890	43.1	2.0	26.3	14.9	13.5
1900	38.0	2.6	28.0	16.9	14.4
1910	32.0	2.9	29.2	19.6	16.3
1920	27.6	3.0	31.7	22.0	15.7
1930	22.6	2.3	29.5	25.9	19.5
1940	18.3	2.2	30.9	25.8	22.8
1950	11.6	1.7	35.7	27.0	23.8

* Excluding parts of the labor force whose industry is unknown.
† Includes also labor force in Electricity and Gas.
‡ Covers the following categories: Professions and Entertainment; Forces; Other Government Services; Private Domestic Service; Other Services.

Source: Adapted from Clark, op. cit., pp. 519-520.

Combined with this great percentage decrease in the labor force in agriculture, there has been, as Table 4-3 shows, a marked increase in other employments. Manufacturing and Construction which employed less than a fifth of the labor force in 1860 accounted for over a third of the total in 1950. Even more striking has been the increase in such occupations as Commerce and Finance, Professions, and similar service industries. The last two categories in Table 4-3 occupied just 20 per cent of the labor force in 1860 and in 1950 were over 50 per cent.[3] There has been, in short, an extremely significant change in the kind of work Americans do as well as in the places where they live.

Nor, thirdly, should we forget the decrease in the *amount* of work Americans do. The expansion of leisure time has been one of the major features of economic development in the United States. Over the century and a half here considered, the work week has fallen from 6 days to 5 and the hours of work from an essentially "sunrise to sunset" regime in agriculture to a standard 8-hour day or less. In the 1870's the average standard work week in the United States was 67 hours. In 1920 it was 46.3 hours. In 1958 it had fallen to 39.2 hours. This shortening of the work week, moreover, does not include the substantial increase in the number of holidays and vacation periods in most occupations. Nor should we forget the fact that, with more young people going on to further education, the age at which individuals enter the working force has been rising. For the first time in the history of the world, leisure—always sought after as a respite from the hard labors of survival—has become something of a problem to be coped with; and, of course, major industries have been rising to meet the need.

Growth in Output and Output Per Capita

Finally, there is the extraordinary expansion of production in the American economy over the past century or more. As we know, it is the increasing volume of material goods per person which more than anything else characterizes modern growth.

This remarkable expansion of total output and the consequent rise in output per capita are displayed in Figs. 4-2 and 4-3 and in Table 4-4. What specifically do these diagrams show? [4]

[3] The categories here used are so broad that they fail to disclose many of the interesting shifts within the categories. Thus, for example, in the category, Transport, Communications, Commerce, and Finance, the Transport and Communications industries have gained only slightly in the percentage of the labor force from 1870 to 1950 and have been declining relatively since 1920. By contrast, employment in Commerce and Finance has grown from 6.5 per cent of the labor force in 1870 to 19.2 per cent in 1950 (a roughly threefold relative increase). Similarly, in the Professions, Government and Other Services category, we have a striking contrast between, say, Private Domestic Service which has been declining relatively (from 7.4 per cent in 1870 to 3.6 per cent in 1950) and Professions and Entertainment which have expanded enormously (from 2.6 per cent in 1870 to 9.0 per cent in 1950). In other words, a more detailed breakdown of occupations gives an even more dramatic picture of the changing pattern of American work than do the broader categories.

[4] In interpreting these diagrams, the student should keep the following points in mind:

1. For total output, the figures cited are those for gross national product (GNP). These GNP figures regularly overstate the economy's net production during any year in that they include investment which is designed simply to replace old, worn-out, or obsolete plant and equipment—i.e., which is not a net addition to the country's capital stock. Estimates for GNP, however, are relatively easier to make than those for the comparable *net* national product and, for a rough measure of growth, we can overlook the difference without too much fear of distortion.

Table 4-4   INCREASE IN GROSS NATIONAL PRODUCT, POPULATION, AND OUTPUT PER CAPITA, UNITED STATES, 1839-1959
(Percentage Increase Per Year)

	Entire Period 1839-1959	40-Year Sub-Periods		
		1839-1879	1879-1919	1919-1959
Gross National Product	3.66	4.31	3.72	2.97
Population	1.97	2.71	1.91	1.30
Output per capita	1.64	1.55	1.76	1.64

Source: Ibid.

1. They show a pronounced, occasionally irregular, upward trend in both total output and output per capita in the American economy over the past 120 years.

2. Total output (GNP) has shown a definite slowing down over this period, its rate of increase having fallen from 4.31 per cent per year (1839-1879) to 3.72 per cent per year (1879-1919) and then to 2.97 per cent per year (1919-1959).

3. Such a decline is not shown, however, in the rate of growth of output per capita which, in the period 1919-1959, grew at 1.64 per cent per year, which was its average annual rate of growth over the period as a whole. The decline in the growth of total output, then, must be attributed to the declining rate of population growth.

4. Finally—and this point should be stressed—this annual rate of growth of output per capita of 1.64 per cent per year is, by any past historical standard, enormously rapid. At such a rate of increase, output per capita doubles about every 43 years. Roughly speaking, this not-very-large-sounding annual rate of increase of 1.64 per cent means a fivefold increase in output per capita per century. To understand the magnitude of such a change, the reader should project this rate into the future. The present average level of family income in the United States is about $6,500 per year (in current dollars). Should the rates of growth of the past century continue over the next, we would have in the year 2060 an average American family income of around $32,500 and this, of course, in terms of present-day purchasing power. If such a development took place, we would witness a society so totally removed from the necessities of life that even the term "affluent" would be much too mild for it.

---

2. These estimates are made in "Constant (1929) Prices." This means that although GNP must be measured in money terms, an attempt has been made to rule out any *fictitious* increases in output deriving from a general increase in prices. Thus, prices in one year (1929) are used as a standard.

3. Finally, the student should remember the series of cautions which were made in our discussion of England's long-run growth (p. 50, above): i.e., that the measurement of growth is a hazardous business and yields only approximate results at best.

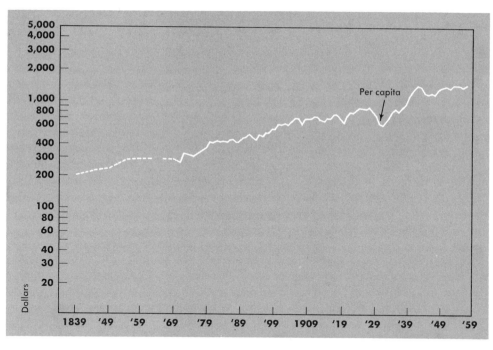

FIG. 4-2 Aggregate Gross National Product in constant (1929) prices, U.S., 1839-1959. (Source: Material presented by Prof. Raymond Goldsmith to the Joint Economic Committee of the U.S. Congress, published in the *Staff Report on Employment, Growth, and Price Levels*, 1959.)

FIG. 4-3 Output per capita in constant (1929) prices, U.S., 1839-1959. (Source: Material presented by Prof. Raymond Goldsmith to the Joint Economic Committee of the U.S. Congress, published in the *Staff Report on Employment, Growth, and Price Levels*, 1959.)

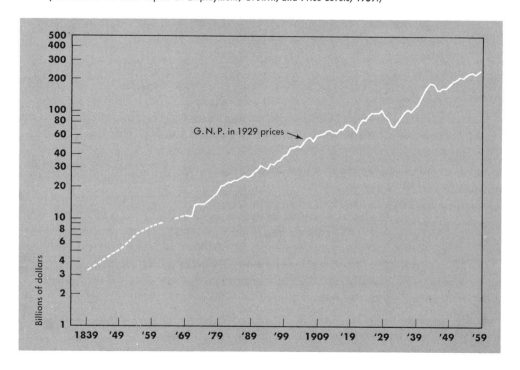

These figures bring home in a concrete way what no amount of general description can suggest: how powerful the engine of modern industrial growth is. Economic development has brought to the average American citizen not only a longer life and more leisure but the most fantastic accumulation of material wealth ever seen in the history of the world.

HOW TO ACCOUNT
FOR THIS GROWTH RECORD

The glories of life, leisure, and abundance are not completely un-alloyed. Reasonable men differ about whether people in the United States are happier, or perhaps even as happy, as they were a century or two centuries ago. Is the affluent society a contented society? For the moral philosopher, the growth of the American economy has posed this unprecedented question.

For the economist, however, the question is slightly different. The trends in the American economy which we have just surveyed are social and economic facts of the first magnitude. As such, and quite apart from value judgments, they require analysis and explanation which it is the business of the social scientist to try to provide. How, then, do we account for this record of American economic growth?

Escaping the "Classical" Dilemma

One first-step way of approaching the problem might be to ask the question: How was the United States able to avoid the kind of dismal fate predicted by the "classical" economists? The country experienced an extraordinary increase in its population over this period; why did the law of diminishing returns fail to dominate the scene?

This question is actually not too difficult to answer. In the first place, it is clear that the growth of American population over the past century and a half, while substantial, did not actually conform to the Malthusian pattern. During most of the period, the birth-rate and the natural rate of increase of the population were actually on the decline. This less-than-maxi-mum rate of population growth, at the very least, gave other growth-producing factors—capital accumulation and technological change—more time to do their work.

Second, it is apparent that during this period the supply of American agricultural land was anything but fixed in quantity. The century following the Revolutionary War saw a vast expansion of the United States' territorial boundaries. The Louisiana Purchase in 1803 virtually doubled the country's land area—and at a cost of less than $12 million. Before the Civil War a further series of acquisitions, cessions, and purchases added well over a million square miles to the nation's lands. Over-all, between 1800 and 1860, the

United States had expanded more than three times geographically, with the consequence that, despite the rapid rate of population growth, the number of persons per square mile rose by the relatively slight margin of from 6.1 to 10.6 over a 60-year span. Indeed, throughout the nineteenth century, we remained essentially a sparsely settled country.

Furthermore, the new land which was brought into cultivation was by no means of "inferior" quality. Ricardo, we recall, had gone on the assumption that a country would begin with superior land and then gradually work its way down to the more inferior grades as population pressures required. In the United States, however, the settlers first cultivated the rocky coast of New England and only later exploited the rich plains and prairies of the Middle West. This fact led one American economist, Henry Charles Carey (1793-1879), to the paradoxical thesis that settlers in a new land would typically begin with poorer lands and gradually move to better—a generalization with rather less to recommend it than Ricardo's, though it happened to be a better "fit" to the special American experience.

Finally, population growth, given the particular features of the American scene, contributed in many *positive* ways to raising the level of output per capita. Thus, for example, population growth was one of the factors responsible for the growth of the large domestic "market" which helped make economies of scale and specialization such a characteristically American reality. It provided a continuing stimulus to increased business investment which helped keep employment reasonably high and thus the actual rate of growth of the economy near its full-employment potentials. Moreover, population growth undoubtedly contributed to the "intangibles" which made the American performance so unique. If the country had remained what it was in the beginning—a small border of people stretched out along the eastern seaboard—would there have been the mobility, the flexibility, the pioneering spirit which typified the country's efforts? And, if not, would the rate of American progress have been anything like what it actually was?

In short, population growth during much of America's history was often a contributing rather than a detracting factor in the matter of the country's level of well-being. The "classical" arrow not only missed the American target; it was flying in the wrong direction.

Factors Making for Increasing Output Per Capita

The above comments fairly well dispose of the "classical" problem, but they by no means give a full explanation of the American growth record. Thus, while it is clear that population growth was *one* of the factors in the making of a broad domestic "market," it is also clear that it was not the *only* factor involved. Similarly, although we can say that the geographical expansion of the United States helped the country escape diminishing returns, we must not overstress this point for the simple reason that, even after the **69** disappearance of the "frontier" in the late nineteenth century, the increase in U.S. output per capita continued at a rapid rate. Clearly, other forces were also at work.

Capital accumulation. One of these forces, as we would expect, was a continuing process of capital accumulation. Since the early days of the republic, there have been vast additions to the American stock of capital. Raymond Goldsmith estimates that the stock of wealth as a whole [5] rose from a little over $1 billion in 1805 to something over $400 billion in 1948. This increase far exceeded the growth of the American population and labor force. In the period from 1879 to 1944, for example, the capital-to-labor ratio in the United States nearly tripled.[6] The average American worker, whether in industry or on the farm, has continuously had more machinery, tools, equipment, buildings, and power to work with. At the same time, the housewife has come to be assisted by an impressive array of devices and mechanical appliances. Over this period, "produced means of production" have been systematically taking over and greatly amplifying the labors of man.

The sources of the great expansion of the American stock of capital have been many. Some of it, particularly in the early stages, was foreign capital. In the 1860's and 1870's, probably half the capital invested in American railroads was foreign. Over-all, the United States was an importer of capital throughout the nineteenth century.

Some of it was mobilized with the assistance of various agencies of the federal, state, and local governments. It was New York State which engineered the construction of the famous Erie Canal. The 9,000-mile southern railway network of 1860 cost $245 million to construct and, of this, over 60 per cent of the financial capital was furnished by public authorities. In countless instances, the government has stepped in either directly or indirectly to provide the means whereby capital could be accumulated for important public needs.

Nevertheless, over this historical span as a whole, it is clear that the primary sources of American capital accumulation were found within the domestic economy and were in the hands of private individuals and institutions. Through direct investment, or through the complex mechanisms of securities markets, banks, and financial intermediaries, individual savings have found their way to private businesses which could use them to expand their physical plant and equipment. Moreover, businesses, farms, and corporations have regularly set aside part of their profits for reinvestment purposes. Such a pattern of "internal financing" has, indeed, increasingly become the dominant form of industrial and capital formation in the United States. In

---

[5] Real reproducible wealth, including consumers durables and government wealth, but excluding military capital (in constant 1929 dollars). Raymond Goldsmith, "The Growth of Reproducible Wealth in the U.S.A. from 1805 to 1950," *Income and Wealth,* Series II (Cambridge: Bowes and Bowes, 1952).

[6] Simon Kuznets, "Long Term Changes in the National Product of the United States of America Since 1870," *Income and Wealth,* Series II, *op. cit.*

the modern American corporation, internal funds—retained profits and depreciation allowances—now provide more than half and sometimes as high as 100 per cent of corporate expenditures on gross investment.

These private, domestic sources of capital accumulation, in turn, can be looked on as largely a reflection of the growth of the American economy. Because this year's output has regularly been greater than last year's, it has been possible for Americans to increase their savings and investment without having thereby to cut into their previous levels of consumption. By the same token, businesses and corporations have found in their own expansion the source of surpluses which could be used for further expansion. Growing production, therefore, has made possible a growing absolute volume of investment over the course of American development.[7]

Transport and the national market. Another of the forces contributing to American growth was the creation during the nineteenth century of a vast national market—the greatest "free trade" area the world has ever known. The European Common Market of recent years is, in part, an attempt to create an analogous economic unity in historically fragmented Europe.

The creation of this national market was a product of many factors— e.g., population growth, the existence of a political and geographic entity, and the general rise in the level of incomes—but no account of its development would be complete without pointing up the importance of improved means of transportation, and especially the railroads.

For sheer magnitude of effort involved, there was nothing in nineteenth-century America that came close to matching the task of constructing the national railroad network. From 1860 to 1900 the number of miles of railway track in operation in the United States increased over six times (from 31,000 to 193,000 miles). In the 1860's and the 1870's, investment in railroad construction was often as high as 10 per cent of the total national product. By 1900 the capital investment in the United States' railroads had reached an over-all total exceeding that of all manufacturing industry put together. This, clearly, was a major economic achievement of nineteenth-century America.

The effects of the railroads were felt in many areas. They brought lowered costs ("external economies") to much of American industry and agriculture. Their construction created greater demands for the products of other sectors of the economy, such as iron and steel. By unifying the country, they broadened the "extent" of the market and made possible specialization

---

[7] The adjective "absolute" is necessary here because it does not seem to be the case that the *percentage* of national output saved and invested has been rising over the years. In the past half-century, at least, this percentage has remained constant or possibly declined. (See, for example: L. R. Klein and R. F. Kosobud, "Some Econometrics of Growth: Great Ratios of Economics," *Quarterly Journal of Economics,* Vol. LXXV, No. 2, May, 1961). In short, American *consumption* of goods and services has been rising as rapidly (and possibly even more rapidly) during this period as the level of national output itself.

by region and growth of large-scale, mass-production industries everywhere. Moreover, in some cases, they were the initiating factor in the growth process. In the Far West, in particular, they were constructed in an economic environment that could not immediately justify their existence—i.e., they were built "ahead of demand." Since the absence of adequate transportation facilities would have impeded the growth of these areas, the construction of the railroads became, in effect, the spearhead of economic progress.

Historians have long known of these varied effects of the railroads on American economic growth but, very recently, there have been serious attempts to *quantify* them. These efforts are part of what some scholars are calling the "new economic history"—economic history written with greater attention to economic theory and especially to its statistical or quantitative component. Whether this approach to economic history qualifies as a new discipline is open to question, but there are a number of partisans, such as the University of Washington's Douglass C. North, who are enthusiastic about its prospects. In the particular case of the railroads, the effect of these recent studies so far has been to qualify some of the more exaggerated claims about the importance of the railroads that past historians have made, but still to leave them a substantial role. Estimates of the saving of resources in the United States attributable to the railroads in the year 1890, for example, range from slightly under 5 per cent to 10-15 per cent of gross national product. These are important social savings, though perhaps not quite as large as were imagined in the past. Similarly, it has been shown that relatively little of the pre-Civil War railroad construction was accomplished "ahead of demand"; still, it has been suggested that the development of certain areas of the Mid-West was made possible in anticipation of the railroads only because of prior railroad development further east: "By the time railroads reached Iowa and Wisconsin, existing economic development justified their construction under private auspices, but only because of prior railroad development in Ohio." [8]

In short, these new studies have made it clear that the effect of the American railroads was more complicated and may have been less in total than was traditionally assumed; but that the railroad was the most important single carrier of economic change in nineteenth-century America still seems a safe conclusion.

The continuing technological revolution. The railroads were a technological innovation, but innovation did not stop with the railroads. A third and final factor to be mentioned as a prime source of American economic growth is the continuing, and still unabated, revolution in technology.

[8] Albert Fishlow, *American Railroads and the Transformation of the Ante-Bellum Economy* (Cambridge: Harvard University Press, 1965), p. 204. Besides Fishlow's account, the reader may consult Robert W. Fogel, *Railroads in American Economic Growth* (Baltimore: Johns Hopkins Press, 1964). Fogel's reduction of the importance of the impact of the American railroads is considerably more than that of Fishlow.

In a sense, of course, American technological progress has been simply a continuation of the process begun in eighteenth-century England which we described in the last chapter. From spinning-jenny and steam engine to railroad, steamship, telegraph, telephone, electric light, automobile, radio, synthetic materials, atomic energy—there has been a more or less unbroken line of major innovations in both the kinds of products Americans produce and in the methods used in producing them. Recent indications are that the process of "automation"—with its potential repercussions on virtually the entire range of commercial and industrial activity—may become the newest member of this family of revolutionary changes.[9]

Although American technological progress is thus linked with the past, it is also clear that the process of technological change has altered over the course of the nation's economic development in certain significant ways. One factor which has created an increasingly favorable environment for technological progress has been the continuing rise in the skills and educational levels of the American people. As recently as 1900, the number of American students in secondary schools was only 11 per cent of the 14-17 age group. By 1960 this percentage had risen to over 80 per cent. Over this same 60-year stretch, enrollments in colleges have risen from around 5 per cent of the college age group to 35 per cent and, in some parts of the country, to as high as 50 per cent. Such changes mean that the American people have become increasingly skilled at creating, adapting, and using new technologies.

Secondly, there has taken place over the course of the past century in America an increased emphasis on systematic research as a means of promoting technological progress. The day of the semi-trained, solitary inventor may or may not be over; what is certain, however, is that, added to his efforts, will be those of the modern research laboratory with its staff of scientists, engineers, and highly trained technicians. This change in emphasis has become strikingly pronounced in recent years. Before the Second World War, total research expenditures in the United States were typically less than $1 billion a year, by 1953 they had risen to $5 billion; by 1960, to $15 billion. Businesses, foundations, universities and, increasingly, the government are all

---

[9] The character of the changes in technology which may be brought about through "automation" is suggested by the definition of Lee A. DuBridge, President of the California Institute of Technology:

"What precisely, then, do we mean by *automation?* In reality, it is simply a new name for the current stage of development of the old process of mechanization. And what characterizes the current stage? Normally, the word is used to describe the multiplicity of electronic devices now used to control industrial processes—to monitor the quality of the product and adjust the machine to correct for deviations, to compute in advance the rate at which materials and parts of particular types should be fed into a complex assembly line, and to continue the process of taking over more and more of the repetitive processes formerly done by hand—and performing them with a delicacy, precision, and speed that human hands could never match. The push-button factory is now nearly a reality; it *is* a reality in certain cases." (Lee A. DuBridge, "Educational and Social Consequences," in John T. Dunlop (ed.), *Automation and Technological Change* [Englewood Cliffs, N.J.: Prentice-Hall, 1962], p. 30.)

involved in the pure and applied scientific research which is the well-spring of technological progress.

The increased emphasis on better education and on systematic, large-scale research is both a cause and a product of the continuing development of the American economy. The kind of technological change which so astonished contemporaries at the time of the English Industrial Revolution has gradually been transformed into a regularized, collective performance whose continued success causes less surprise than would its failure. "Progress is our most important product" is not only the slogan of one American firm; it is also a deep statement about an economy which is beginning to "produce" new technology in the same way it produces bushels of wheat and yards of cloth.[10]

THE "RESIDUAL" IN AMERICAN GROWTH

These, then, have been some of the forces which account for the remarkable growth of American production over the past century or more. In the background lie the favorable political, cultural, and historical circumstances with which the country began. In the foreground lies the combination of geographical expansion, population growth, and improved means of transport which created a great national market; a persistent rise in the amount of capital per worker; and the continuing and increasingly systematic search for improved methods of technology.

It would be useful if, at this point, we could probe somewhat more deeply into the mechanism of American growth and arrange this array of factors according to some hierarchy of importance. As we know from Chapter 1, the attempt to do this has been made with reference to what is sometimes called the "residual." Although these studies are necessarily rough, and are confined to a comparatively recent period in our history, their uniformity of conclusion is fairly encouraging. That conclusion has been that only a limited percentage of American growth can be accounted for by the sheer quantitative increase in factor inputs (labor and capital) and that a very healthy percentage is due to a "residual" term representing increased output per unit of input.

This conclusion is useful as a starting point in our analysis, but what we should *really* like to know is something about the content of this residual item.

[10] One of the interesting questions which this change in attitude raises is: What now happens to the function of the *entrepreneur* or *innovator* which the late Professor Schumpeter emphasized so strongly? If a society becomes completely adjusted to the process of technological change, then the function of innovation and *leadership* could conceivably become increasingly *less* important. This, indeed, was Schumpeter's own view. In highly developed societies he foresaw the possibility that progress would become completely routinized. In such a society the entrepreneurial function might easily become, as he put it, "obsolete." See Joseph A. Schumpeter, *Capitalism, Socialism and Democracy* (New York: Harper, 1950), pp. 131-134.

To say that it is "technical progress" is insufficient since, as we already know, this term must be made to bear an unhealthy burden of heterogeneous items.

The breaking down of the "residual" into its component parts and assigning appropriate weights to each is an immensely difficult task, but it is a highly important one and at least the first steps have been taken. E. F. Denison's results for the 1929-1957 period are summarized in Table 4-5.

Table 4-5 SPECIFIC ACCOUNTING FOR THE SOURCES
OF U.S. GROWTH, 1929-1957

	Percentage Points in Growth Rate
Real National Income	2.93
Increase in Total Inputs	2.00
Labor input (adjusted for quality change)	1.57
Employment	1.00
Hours (annual)	−0.53
Effect of shorter hours on quality of a man-year's work	0.33
Education	0.67
Other	0.10
Capital input	0.43
Non-farm residential structures	0.05
Other structures and equipment	0.28
Other	0.10
Increase in Output per Unit of Input	0.93
Advance in knowledge	0.58
Economies of scale	0.34
Industry shift from agriculture	0.05
Other	−0.04

Source: Denison, op. cit., Table 32 (adapted). Notice the high percentage of output growth attributed to the combined impact of "Education" and "Advance in knowledge" during this period.

The attempt here is to account for the "residual" by attributing part of it to the improved quality of the labor input and another part of it to various items such as "advance in knowledge." It goes without saying that, at the present moment, these estimates are far more art than science.

The main upshot of this range of work so far has been to give economists a rather different view of the growth process than was common in the nineteenth century or even in the early decades of the twentieth. There was always a natural tendency among students and scholars to concentrate on the more tangible factors in growth such as the accumulation of tools, machines and equipment. Such accumulation of tools is, of course, a vital part of economic growth. But even *more* vital has been the growth of skills and knowledge and the facts that we are constantly using different methods of production to produce different products and to distribute them in different ways.

THE FUTURE:
SELF-SUSTAINED GROWTH FOREVER?

These studies also have an important bearing on the question of the future of American economic development. Will American growth continue at the same rate in the years ahead as in years past? Will it accelerate? Slow down? What does our analysis suggest about possible future trends? Like all questions about the future, these lead us into matters which are necessarily highly conjectural. Nevertheless, there are a few general comments which are worth noting.

If we look at *past* American development, it is clear that what we have called the "self-sustaining" elements in the growth process have been far more important than the "self-limiting" elements. Given the abundance of American resources, the law of diminishing returns, for example, had a negligible impact on the country's development. In contrast, the process of growth, by helping to create a national market, by providing sources of capital, and by stimulating a continuing search for technological improvement, generally strengthened the factors making for increased production and living standards. In this sense growth was stimulating further growth in the "self-sustaining" manner we have described in an earlier chapter.

If, now, we proceed from this picture to that of America in the 1960's, we can notice that certain changes have taken place. For one thing, the "frontier" has long since disappeared. Few economists believe that resource limitations are likely to be very serious ones for the American economy for the foreseeable future; nevertheless, insofar as the "frontier" was a generally favorable factor in earlier American development, the change is clearly not on the positive side.

Similarly, it seems unlikely that a further growth of the national market either through increased population, better transport, or a continuing increase in the general level of production, will have quite such favorable effects in the future as it did in the past. This point is, of course, a good deal a matter of opinion. No one knows what new economies of scale and specialization may become feasible under some future and more advanced technology, nor how dependent such economies may be on a still further enlargement of the American (and international) market. Still, it seems rather optimistic to assume that such future effects would be of the same order of magnitude as those which the combination of railroads, expanding population and resources, and rising incomes produced in the last century.

When we turn next to the matter of capital accumulation, we find that the picture is rather mixed. Continuing economic growth will undoubtedly facilitate an increasing level of investment in the future as it has in the past. On the other hand, because American consumption has tended to keep pace with the growth of American production, there is no reason to expect investment to rise as a *percentage* of total production over the years ahead; if anything, present indicators point the other way.[11] All this is complicated by the fact that the future course of capital formation in the United States is likely to be substantially influenced by the actions of government, both in their indirect effects on private business investment and in their direct effects on taxing and spending and thus altering the amount of saving and investment in the public sector. In short, the future here is extremely difficult to predict. What we can say, however, is that present trends give us no reason for believing that capital accumulation will contribute *more* substantially to future growth than it did to past. At the moment, it would seem that it would take some doing for the American economy even to *match* its past performance in this respect.

In all these respects, then, the future growth prospects of the American economy, as compared with the past, would appear either slightly less or only equally favorable at best. The balance so far would seem to point to a slowing down of the potential rate of growth of the economy.

But this, of course, is without taking technological progress into account. And here it would appear—or, at least, it can be argued—that the prospects for future advance are as promising and, in many respects, even more promising than they were in the past. The fact that systematic, specialized, large-scale research is essentially a new phenomenon—taking root in the United States only within the past 15 or 20 years—suggests that the American economy may actually be at the *beginning* rather than at the *end* of the period of epochal technological changes. Economists are now talking about the "new industry of discovery." The rate of advance in pure, applied, and technological science has continued unabated and may, if anything, be accelerating.

This factor alone could easily shift the balance. If American technological progress continues at a vigorous pace, then the prospects for continuing American growth are likely to remain quite favorable even if the other contributing factors are somewhat less promising than in the past. This is simply to repeat the main burden of the recent studies of American development—namely, that of all the forces which produce modern growth, the one which carries the greatest responsibility and gives the greatest thrust is the continuing technological revolution. If, as seems more than possible, the progress in American technology remains strong—conceivably even gaining in strength as it goes along—then there does not seem to be any *fundamental* reason why future American performance should not match, maybe even surpass, the past.

Needless to say, this conclusion is no more than a conjecture. Moreover, it is fairly limited in its scope. It does not imply, for example, that the future

[11] See the reference in Footnote 7, p. 71.

rate of growth of the American economy will be as fast as Americans may feel they want, or require. Furthermore, it does not even touch on the question of whether a high rate of future growth, though *potentially* achievable, will *actually* be achieved. This actual achievement would depend not only on the ability of the economy to *supply* an ever-increasing volume of production but also on the way in which consumer, business, and government *demand* grew in response to that increased availability of goods and services. As we have said before: In a market economy, the mere ability to produce goods is never a sufficient warrant for expecting that the goods will actually be produced.[12]

What these speculations do suggest, however, is that there do not at the moment appear to be any fundamental obstacles preventing the American economy from supplying a continuing increase in output per capita, and at rates comparable to those of the past. One might even hazard the guess that if the growth of output per capita in the United States begins to decline in the future, it will in all likelihood be because our interest in the growth process has been diminished by its success. We may, after all, eventually tire of the continued pursuit and achievement of material abundance.

SUMMARY

Of all the major countries in the world, the United States presents the most dramatic example of the effects and potentialities of modern economic growth. The American achievement, accomplished in an environment favored by geographical, historical, and political circumstances, has yet to be matched by any other nation.

The economic development of the United States over the past century and a half has either produced or been accompanied by a variety of pronounced changes in the basic conditions of American life. One dramatic change has been in the size of the country, population increasing by over 30 times in the period 1800-1960. A major element in this population growth was a persistent fall in the American death-rate; the life expectancy of Americans, for example, has increased by 75 per cent in the last century. But there were equally dramatic changes in the location, type, and quantity of work in which Americans were engaged. During the course of this period, Americans moved from rural to urban areas, they shifted from farming to manufacturing and increasingly to trade and professional services, and they worked much *less*—the amount of leisure enjoyed by Americans has increased enormously.

Finally, American development was characterized by a massive increase

[12] Thus, many of the measures taken in recent years to accelerate the American rate of growth have been wholly or partly directed to insuring that the growth of aggregate demand in the economy keeps pace with the growth in aggregate supply. The tax-cut of 1964 is a notable example. It might be added that such measures appear to have been successful. In the late 1950's, American growth in GNP was less than 2½ per cent per year; from 1961 to 1965, however, it was over 4½ per cent per year.

in the country's total output and output per capita. As population growth has slowed down over the decades, the growth of total output has slowed down as well, but the rise in output per capita has continued unabated. At a rate of between 1½ per cent and 2 per cent per year, this persistent increase in output per capita has brought to Americans the highest average standard of living ever witnessed in the history of the world. It has created the "affluent" society.

Accounting for this record of growth is, of course, a most difficult matter. Nevertheless, a few general points can be made: In the first place, it is clear that "classical" fears of diminishing returns were quite inappropriate as applied to the American situation. Population growth was not so rapid, resources neither so fixed nor scarce, and the potentialities of a big market not so limited as the Ricardo-Malthus analysis might have led one to believe. Over-all, population growth during much of American history probably contributed to a rise rather than a decline in the average level of well-being.

Secondly, there were a number of positive factors which clearly contributed greatly to the increase in American output per capita: (1) There was a vast amount of capital accumulation resulting in a persistent increase in the amount of capital per worker. (2) There was the growth of the national market and spread of the railroads which helped unify the country and were sometimes the initiating force in regional development. (3) There was a continuing process of technological change which stemmed initially from the English Industrial Revolution but was increasingly favored by higher standards of education in the country and the beginnings of systematic, large-scale research.

All these factors were interrelated. Nevertheless, recent studies suggest that during the past half century a large percentage of American growth must be attributed to increased output per unit of inputs (the "residual"). The attempt to break this "residual" into its component parts is extremely difficult but preliminary efforts to do so suggest the great importance of education and the advancement of knowledge in the American achievement, at least in recent decades. Economists now view growth not simply as an increase in labor and capital supply but, very significantly, as a continuing process of technological change.

These conclusions have a bearing on the future potentials of American economic growth. In scanning the future, we find that the one factor which seems at least as favorable as and possibly even more favorable than it was historically is technological progress. Since this factor seems to be a highly important element in the growth-process, there appears to be no fundamental reason to expect that America's productive achievements will be less in the future than they were in the past.

The Problems

of the Underdeveloped Countries

CHAPTER FIVE

In the age of jet aircraft, the time distance which separates the United States from one of the underdeveloped countries of Asia, Africa, or Latin America is only a matter of hours. Measured in economic distance, the gap is more like that between the present and the Dark Ages. Over the past century the time distance has been constantly narrowing; during the same period the economic distance has become immeasurably wider. The United States and the other economically advanced countries of the world have been growing steadily richer at rates never before dreamed of. The poor countries of the world, with a few exceptions, have remained poor; in many cases, conditions have notably deteriorated. It is all told in the Bible:

> For unto every one that hath shall be given, and he shall have abundance; but from him that hath not shall be taken away even that which he hath. (St. Matthew, xxv, 29)

The story of the "hath nots" is the story of the modern underdeveloped countries.

MEANING OF ECONOMIC UNDERDEVELOPMENT

One cannot, of course, divide the world quite so neatly **80** into economically advanced countries, on one hand, and underdeveloped countries, on the other. We have a whole spectrum of degrees of development depending on when a country embarked on the path of modern growth and on the progress it has achieved. From the point of view of the United States, the Soviet Union is still, in most respects, an underdeveloped nation. Much the same can be said of Europe in general. For that matter, if we are thinking of growth *potentialities,* the United States with its continuing favorable prospects is itself an "underdeveloped" country.

Even when we limit our attention to the definitely poorer countries of the world, moreover, we still find a great variety of conditions. Some are much poorer than others. Some are growing; some are not. In a country like India there is a civilization which is, in many respects, older than that of the West. By contrast, in certain regions of Africa and Oceania we find a tribal organization of the most primitive kind. In some countries, such as Ceylon, Colombia, Peru, and Indonesia, there is a relatively rich endowment of natural resources; in others, such as Jordan and Yemen, the poverty of resources may be a major deterrent to development. There are, moreover, very significant differences in the densities of population as between these various countries. Brazil, for example, has roughly 30 times as much land per capita as does Taiwan. Broadly speaking, Africa and Latin America tend to be relatively underpopulated while Asia is heavily overpopulated, but even here there are important exceptions to the rule.

In short, the problem is not one of a single situation but of a whole complex of different situations in which the obstacles to progress are likely to be extremely varied. What unites this group and makes the notion of "underdeveloped countries" a meaningful one, however, is that all these countries have just begun to experience, or have yet to experience, the phenomenon of rapid economic growth which has become so characteristic in the economically advanced nations. In one way or another, they are all still wrapped up in what we have called the problem of "getting started." While the nations of Europe, North America, and Australasia were one by one entering the development race, these countries remained at the post. The result has been persistent, grinding poverty in a world where affluence was, at last, becoming conceivable.

HOW POOR IS POOR?

Poverty means one thing to an American wage-earner; it means quite a different thing to the beggar in the streets of Calcutta. How can we measure in quantitative terms the degree of poverty existing in the underdeveloped countries of the modern world?

The problems we encounter here are very similar to those we have mentioned in connection with the measurement of long-term economic growth. Accurate statistics are seldom available; many of the relevant items are all but impossible to include; the differences in the kinds and relative quantities of goods produced in a poor country as opposed to a more advanced country make international comparisons extremely difficult; and so on.

Table 5-1 PER-CAPITA OUTPUT IN 1957 (Converted to U.S. Dollars by Means of Foreign Exchange Rates)

Group A: Annual Per-Capita Output of $0-$100 (Includes 49.7% of the World's Population)

America	Asia and Middle East	Africa
Falkland Islands	Pakistan	Ruandi-Urundi
and Bolivia	Sarawak	Somaliland
Greenland	Thailand	South West Africa
	Truncial Oman	Span. Guinea
Asia and Middle East	Vietnam (North and South)	Sudan
Afghanistan	Yemen	Tanganyika
Bhutan		Togoland
Brunei	Africa	Uganda
Burma	Angola	Others
Cambodia	Belgian Congo	
China	Br. Cameroons	Oceania
Gaza Strip	Eritrea and Ethiopia	Australian Oceania
India	Fr. Equatorial Africa	Br. Oceania
Maldive Islands	Fr. West Africa	Fr. Oceania
Mongolian People's	Gambia	New Zealand Oceania
Republic	Kenya	U.S. Oceania
Muscat and Oman	Liberia	Nauru
Nepal	Libya	New Hebrides
Neth. New Guinea	Madagascar	New Guinea
North Borneo	Mozambique	Pacific Islands (U.S.)
North Korea	Nigeria	Western Samoa (N.Z.)

Group B: Annual Per-Capita Output of $101-$300 (Includes 17.1% of the World's Population)

Latin America	Latin America	Asia and Middle East
Brazil	Virgin Islands	Jordan
British Guiana	West Indies (other)	Korea (South)
Br. Honduras		Macao
Colombia	Europe	Philippines
Dominican Republic	Albania	Port. India
Ecuador	Andorra	Port. Timor
El Salvador	Faeroe Islands	Ryukyu Islands
Fr. Guiana	Portugal	Saudi Arabia
Guadeloupe	Spain	Turkey
Guatemala	Yugoslavia	U. A. R.
Haiti		
Honduras	Asia and Middle East	
Martinique	Aden	Africa
Mexico	Bahrein	Algeria
Neth. Antilles	Ceylon	Fr. Cameroons
Nicaragua	China (Taiwan)	Ghana
Paraguay	Hong Kong	Mauritius
Peru	Indonesia	Morocco
St. Pierre and Miquelon	Iran	Rhodesia and Nyasaland
Surinam	Iraq	Tunisia

Group C: Annual Per-Capita Output of $301-$600 (Includes 18% of the World's Population)

Latin America	Asia and Middle East	Europe
Argentina	Japan	Greece
Canal Zone	Malaya	Hungary
Chile	Singapore	Iceland
Costa Rica	Lebanon	Ireland
Cuba	Cyprus	Italy
Federation of West Indies		Malta
Panama	Europe	Poland
Puerto Rico	Bulgaria	Rumania
Uruguay	E. Germany	San Marino
	Gibraltar	U. S. S. R.
Africa		
Union of South Africa		

Group D: Annual Per-Capita Output of $601-$1,200 (Includes 7.5% of the World's Population)

Latin America	Europe	Europe
Venezuela	Belgium	Monaco
	Czechoslovakia	Netherlands
Asia and the Middle East	Denmark	Norway
Israel	Finland	United Kingdom
	France	
Europe	W. Germany	
Austria	Liechtenstein	

Group E: Annual Per-Capita Output of $1,200 and Above (Includes 7.7% of the World's Population)

	Average Per-Capita Output		Average Per-Capita Output
America		Asia	
United States		Kuwait *	$2,722
and Canada	$2,521	Qatar *	
Europe			
Luxemburg	$1,399	Oceania	
Sweden ·		Australia	
Switzerland		and New Zealand	$1,315

* The unexpected appearance of Kuwait and Qatar in Group E can be explained in one word: oil!

Since these figures on output per capita are converted to U.S. dollars by means of foreign exchange rates they tend to overstate the differences between the economically advanced countries and the underdeveloped countries. Nevertheless, the gap is so great that even when a generous correction is made, the differences in comparative living standards are still enormous. All the countries in Groups A and B must be considered seriously "underdeveloped." Together, these two groups constitute 66.8% or about two-thirds of the world's population.

Source: Hagen: "Some Facts about Income Levels and Economic Growth," op. cit.

Despite these problems, however, various attempts have been made to estimate the levels of output per capita in the underdeveloped countries of the world as compared with their more favorably situated neighbors. The truth is that the differences are *so* enormous that even the most defective measuring sticks could not fail to detect them.

In Table 5-1, some estimates of output per capita in the various countries of the world for the year 1957 are presented. These particular estimates have been converted to United States dollars by means of the foreign exchange rates of the countries involved. As it turns out, this method of conversion has the defect of *over*emphasizing the gap between rich and poor nations—mainly because the foreign exchange rates reflect the prices of internationally traded goods which, in most underdeveloped countries, are more expensive than goods consumed domestically. Thus, a mental correction must be made to a picture which presents things as worse than they really are.[1]

Still, when all is said and done, the striking thing which emerges from Table 5-1 is *how very low* the level of output per capita in most of the world's countries is. According to these estimates, roughly half the world's population produces less than $100 of output per person per year—in contrast to the United States and Canada where the figure is $2,521. Another 17 per cent of the world's population has an annual output per capita of between $100 and $300. Together, these two groups of countries present us with a clear problem of economic underdevelopment. In terms of population, they comprise two-thirds of the world. In terms of geography, they include most of Latin America, virtually all of Asia and Africa, and a few countries within Europe. Even if the estimates of output per capita in these regions were low by two, three or even four times, the central conclusion would remain—two-thirds of the world is extremely poor and a sizable fraction is living in circumstances which can only be called desperate.

THE DEMAND FOR DEVELOPMENT

Poverty, even desperate poverty, is not a new phenomenon in many of these countries. It may be true, as some economists have argued, that the industrial development of the economically advanced countries has sometimes had adverse effects on the standards of living of the poorer countries;[2] but, whether true or not, this is not the essential explanation of why these countries are poor. The fact is that they were poor at the time of the English

---

[1] For a discussion of this problem, see Everett E. Hagen, "Some Facts about Income Levels and Economic Growth," *Review of Economics and Statistics,* Vol. XLII, No. 1, February, 1960.

[2] Thus, for example, Professor Gunnar Myrdal speaks of the "backwash effects" of the growth of the industrial economies on the industries of the poorer countries which were unable to compete with their more efficient competitors. Also, there were the many instances where colonial governments actually took measures to stifle the development of indigenous industries. See Gunnar Myrdal, *Economic Theory and Under-Developed Regions* (London: Duckworth, 1957). It would be a mistake, however, to think that *all* the effects of Western development were in this negative direction. Even colonial occupation often brought advantages as well as disadvantages. It was, in fact,

a very mixed picture.

Industrial Revolution; in most cases, they have been poor since the dawn of history. Poverty is an ancient, not a modern, condition.

What is new in the modern underdeveloped countries, then, is not the fact that they are poor but the fact that they have become *aware* of being poor and have grown increasingly determined to *do something* about it. This awareness and determination, in turn, are largely a product of the exposure of these countries to the economic achievements of the industrialized world. There has been what economists sometimes call an international "demonstration effect." [3] Because of the colonial interpenetration of the East by the West during the nineteenth century, and because of the dramatic improvements in the means of communications in the twentieth, the poor countries have had a constant "demonstration" of the economic superiority of Western ways. The sharp contrast in standards of living between the economically advanced peoples and their own has not escaped them. On the contrary, it has led to constantly growing demands for rapid development at no matter what the cost.

This insistence on quick progress has given rise to many problems. Politically, it has often been associated with a violent rejection of the ways of the former colonial powers and a susceptibility to slogans and ideologies which find scapegoats in the past and give easy promises for the future. Moreover, it sometimes poses obstacles to the achievement of the very economic development which is desired. In some underdeveloped countries, the emulation of Western achievements has led governments to adopt many of the social-security and other "welfare" measures which, in the case of the economically advanced nations, came only at a very late stage of their forward progress. A poor country, in trying to do more than it can afford, can easily sap the strength of the forces which might make for permanent economic development.

In the final analysis, however, it should be said that this awakened desire for improvement is the main driving force capable of dislodging the modern underdeveloped country from its rut of ancient poverty. Without such an awakening, the tense problems of economic development might disappear. But it would not be poverty that had disappeared—only the will to overcome it.

---

[3] The term "demonstration effect" was originally developed by Harvard University's James S. Duesenberry (*Income, Saving and the Theory of Consumer Behavior* [Cambridge: Harvard University Press, 1949]), to explain how consumers might be affected by the living standards of other consumers within the domestic economy. This general notion was applied to the international sphere by the late Ragnar Nurkse in his important book, *Problems of Capital Formation in Underdeveloped Areas* (New York: Oxford University Press, 1953). The idea is that awareness of higher living standards elsewhere may bring pressure for an increase in one's own living standards. Of course, a simple desire for better living does not necessarily *bring* better living. Indeed, Nurkse feared that poor countries in trying to raise their immediate consumption levels might actually impede the process of long-run capital formation, and therefore, long-run growth. **85**

THE OBSTACLES TO DEVELOPMENT

If the demand for economic development in the modern under-developed countries is great, so also are the obstacles to its achievement. In fact, most economists believe that the problems of "getting started" in these countries may be much more difficult than those which faced the developing nations of the nineteenth century.

In a way this is a rather surprising conclusion because the modern underdeveloped country does have at its disposal a most potent instrument of growth—namely, the whole apparatus of modern technology which has been developed in the industrial countries. The potentialities for "borrowing" techniques are now enormous. It is typical—and a little paradoxical—that a country like India, with an output per capita of less than $100 a year, already has her own Atomic Energy Commission. With a similar level of income, China already has the atomic bomb.

However, as we saw in our discussion of the "late-comers" of the nineteenth century, there are often difficulties as well as advantages in following after. And, in the case of the modern underdeveloped countries, these difficulties, plus a variety of special circumstances, have created what often seem to be virtually insurmountable obstacles to progress. Here are a few of the problems which may make the process of "getting started" more difficult for these countries than it was for their predecessors:

1. *The difficulty of adapting Western technology.* Advanced Western technology, on which most hopes for progress are pinned, is by no means ideally suited to the conditions of the typical underdeveloped country. By and large, this technology has evolved along lines appropriate to the conditions of the countries which created it, meaning that it uses (relatively) little labor and a great deal of capital, and depends in its operations on the existence of a reservoir of skilled labor and technically trained personnel. Such a technology is quite inappropriate to most underdeveloped countries where: (a) labor is abundant or super-abundant; (b) capital is extremely scarce; and (c) there is often an acute shortage of skilled labor and management. Ideally, the underdeveloped countries would employ a technology which is neither the Western technology of a century ago (which is defective) nor the most modern Western technology (which is adapted to a different kind of economic context), but a *third* technology which consists of an adaptation of modern methods to the special conditions of the underdeveloped world. Despite some efforts in this direction, however, this third technology does not really exist. Lacking it, the modern underdeveloped country typically tries to import the "latest" Western methods, with the consequence that it faces acute shortages in certain areas (capital and trained personnel) while it has idle surpluses in others (large numbers of unemployed, unskilled workers).

2. *Lack of preparation for an industrial revolution.* In the nineteenth century, industrial revolutions were launched primarily in Europe or in countries linked with Europe where the social and economic groundwork was reasonably well-laid. In the typical modern underdeveloped country, an attempt is being made to accomplish simultaneously both the industrial revolution and the preparations *for* such a revolution. The difficulties here are sometimes extreme, particularly in the political sphere. Consider, for example, the political unrest and frequent changes of government in the Congo since independence. Even the economically hopeful country of Nigeria has recently been subjected to considerable interregional strains. In Southeast Asia, Indonesia has just experienced a major political upheaval and bloodbath. In many underdeveloped countries a complete social and political revolution is required while the industrial revolution is getting underway. In general, the lack of prior preparation means that these countries are economically poorer than their nineteenth-century predecessors; it means that their agricultural and commercial sectors have not developed to the point where they can easily sustain rapid industrial progress; it means, above all, that there has been little or no time for their institutions and value systems to adapt themselves to modern economic change. A sharp desire for material betterment, a willingness to work hard and in a regular, punctual manner, an awareness of the future benefits of present sacrifices—these attitudes may be the prerequisites of economic growth; yet they may be largely absent in many underdeveloped countries.

3. *Population problems.* Most modern underdeveloped countries face population problems of a different and much more serious sort than did the nations of the West a century ago. Partly this is a matter of the rate of increase of population; partly it is a matter of population density in relation to land and other resources.

As we know, the modern underdeveloped countries have undergone a "public health revolution" which has made possible a fall in the death-rate and consequently rapid population growth even in the absence of substantial economic development. In India and China—comprising over a third of the world's population—population is now increasing at 2 per cent or over per year. In Latin America the rate of increase is between 2½ per cent and 3 per cent. These are very rapid rates of increase and they pose serious difficulties for poor countries in which the rate of capital formation tends to be low. The danger is that such capital as is accumulated may simply go into spreading a larger quantity of tools over a larger number of people without actually raising per-capita productivity. This problem is likely to continue, moreover, because death-rates in these countries are still high relative to the economically advanced countries and therefore may continue to fall in the future.

Furthermore, the increase in population is all the *more* serious in those countries where population is already dense in relation to land and other resources. Generally speaking, this is the situation in Asia, where the great majority of the poverty-stricken of the world are located. In many of these Asiatic countries, population is already pressing against the available cultivable land in a thoroughly "classical" manner. In some extreme cases, such as Java, there are well over 1,000 persons per square mile. Under such circumstances, population growth is not a stimulant to development, as it was in the United States, but a depressant. Because of the lack of industrial capital, the growing labor force cannot find jobs in the city and therefore adds itself to the already congested rural areas. Rapid population growth in such "labor surplus" economies may mean that despite the attempts to increase industrial employment, the absorption rate is insufficient, and that open and disguised unemployment increase as a percentage of the labor force—the reverse of successful development.[4]

4. *The international context.* Finally, many economists would add that the modern underdeveloped countries face a rather different and generally less favorable international environment than did the developing countries of the nineteenth century. Often this problem is put in terms of the degree to which private investors in the economically advanced countries are willing to provide sources of capital to their poorer neighbors. In the nineteenth century, British foreign investment flowed freely and massively to the then developing areas of the world. By contrast, in the twentieth century, the flow of private capital from rich to poor countries has been a mere trickle in relation to their needs. In the case of the United States, much of our private foreign investment goes to economically advanced countries (e.g., Canada and Western Europe), and a large fraction of the rest is devoted to extractive products, like oil, where the impact on the over-all development of the poor country may be relatively limited.

In general, and in part due to the attitudes of the underdeveloped countries themselves, the current climate for private foreign investment is a rather unfavorable one. With former colonial abuses in mind and with a strong upsurge of nationalistic feeling, many of these countries have effectively restricted both the kinds and the terms of investment open to foreign investors. Even where restrictions do not exist, the danger of nationalization and expropriation is always present. Under such circumstances, American investors will often prefer to employ their capital in more familiar and secure surroundings, particularly when—as, for example, in the case of the Common Market countries—economic progress is continually creating new and favorable opportunities.

[4] Estimates of the extent of "disguised unemployment" vary from country to country and economist to economist. Some observers find evidence of situations where 25 per cent, 30 per cent or even as high as 45 per cent of the rural labor force is contributing little or nothing to rural output. Other economists believe such estimates are exaggerated. For a background discussion of the "labor surplus" economy, see Chapter 2.

To a degree, of course, this deficiency is made up for by the increase in intergovernmental aid—loans and grants from the United States and other countries and international agencies—which has taken place during the past 15 years. Because of the comparative lack of private investment, however, the gap to be filled by these aid programs is a very substantial one.

These, then, are some of the special problems which a modern underdeveloped country faces in its attempts to achieve rapid growth. The advantage of having a ready-made foreign technology is considerably qualified by the fact that that technology makes severe demands on its scarce supplies of capital and skilled labor and management. It faces the herculean task of transplanting an industrial revolution into a social and economic context which has not naturally been prepared for it. It suffers from acute population problems. And its hopes for foreign assistance have come to rest more and more on the largess of friendly governments and international organizations.

This list, of course, does not include anything like all the obstacles to development which these countries face. It merely suggests some of the ways in which the problem of "getting started"—difficult enough at best—may be even *more* difficult for the modern underdeveloped countries than it was for those who accomplished the breakthrough in the nineteenth century. We can now understand why many economists feel that the "vicious circles of poverty" may be particularly "vicious" in these countries and why the initial push may have to be an especially big one.

THE SCALE OF POSSIBLE DEVELOPMENT

The combination of an intense demand for rapid growth and the existence of severe obstacles to growth is the source of profound social and political tensions in many modern underdeveloped countries. For the student of economic development, it raises a number of interesting and difficult problems. Can these demands for growth actually be met? Have these countries any reasonable hope of closing or at least narrowing the gap between themselves and the economically advanced countries? What, realistically, is the scale of possible future development that may be achieved in the underdeveloped areas?

Such questions have no definite answers, but they do raise certain points which it is well to keep in mind. In the first place, it should be said that experience, both past and present, suggests that modern economic growth can be launched in a wide variety of apparently unlikely contexts. The achievement of Japan during the past 75 years is an historical case in point. In recent years we have the fact that many of the underdeveloped countries have, indeed, shown an acceleration in their rates of progress. To take a few examples from the past 15 years:

Table 5-2   RATES OF GROWTH OF MODERN
UNDERDEVELOPED COUNTRIES

| Nation | Average Annual Rate of Growth of GNP | |
	1950-1960	1960-1964
Ceylon	6.1 [a]	2.2
Chile	3.6	3.5
Colombia	4.6	4.4 [b]
Ecuador	4.9	4.0
Guatemala	3.8	6.1
Honduras	3.5	4.0 [b]
Jamaica	7.7 [c]	4.0
Korea, Rep. of	4.8 [c]	6.2
Malawi	4.0 [d]	1.0 [b]
Paraguay	2.7	3.5
Peru	4.9	6.4
Philippines	4.5 [e]	4.1
Sudan	5.0 [e]	6.9 [f]
Taiwan	7.9 [g]	7.1 [b]
Uruguay	0.0 [c]	—0.1 [b]
Zambia	8.2 [e]	3.4

[a] 1958-1960   [e] 1955-1960
[b] 1960-1963   [f] 1960-1962
[c] 1953-1960   [g] 1951-1960
[d] 1954-1960

Source: United Nations, Department of Economic and Social Affairs, *Statistical Yearbook, 1965*, pp. 562-564.

These rates, after all, compare quite favorably with that of the United States (a little over 3½ per cent) during most of its historic development. Some countries are doing better than others and, of course, the per-capita rate of advance is lessened by dint of the great population upsurge. Nevertheless, in the underdeveloped world as a whole, the past 15 years have seen definite forward strides as compared to times past.

Having said this, however, we should counter with a second point which is this: Any hope that these countries might have of closing or even seriously narrowing the economic gap which separates them from a country like the United States is—at least for the foreseeable future—an unrealistic one. This point is brought home very forcibly by some arithmetic calculations which were made a few years ago by the Economic Commission for Latin America.[5] These calculations, it should be remembered, pertain to Latin America where the average level of per-capita output is already considerably higher than that of Africa or Asia.

[5] UN Department of Economic and Social Affairs, *Analyses and Projections of Economic Development: A Study Prepared by the Economic Commission for Latin America: I.* "An Introduction to the Technique of Programming" (New York: U.N., 1955). Cf. discussion in Benjamin Higgins, *Economic Development* (New York: Norton, 1959), pp. 432-440.

The Commission asked, in effect, how long it would take, under various assumptions, for output per capita in Latin America as a whole to reach a level equal to *one-third* of the United States level. Assuming that output per capita in Latin America were to rise by a healthy 2.4 per cent per year, they found that it would take 42 years for it to equal one-third of the present U.S. output per capita. But that, of course, is the *present* level of U.S. output per capita. If one is thinking in terms of narrowing the gap, one would have to take into account the fact that the level of U.S. output per capita would *also* be continuing to rise during this period. On the assumption that U.S. output per capita were to rise at the rate of 2 per cent per year, the Commission found that it would take *252 years* for the level of output per capita in Latin America to reach one-third of the then current U.S. output per capita!

Needless to say, these assumed rates of increase for both the United States and Latin America are arbitrary, and the conclusions therefore are necessarily arbitrary too. Nevertheless, the calculations do bring out clearly the scope of the problem facing the modern underdeveloped countries. For all practical purposes, and barring completely unforeseen circumstances, there is no reason to expect that the gap between the highly advanced and economically underdeveloped countries will be closed or even appreciably narrowed over the course of the next century or more. In the year 2060 there will still be rich nations and poor. Or, if there are not, it will most likely be because of political and military circumstances, not the economic.

All of which suggests that the goals of most underdeveloped countries must be on a considerably more modest scale. This is not a counsel of despair, however. For certainly *the* most important goal of any poor country must be the removal of the extremes of poverty which shorten, cripple, and undermine the value of human life. The goal of "catching up" with the West may be morally defensible, but it is not crucial. What *is* crucial is that children should not die of malnutrition and exposure and that adults should enjoy life with that minimum of health, comfort, and leisure necessary to physical and mental peace. And this goal, given modern technology, should lie within the realm of the possible. Its achievement, moreover, is to the interest of every nation, rich or poor. For, as the former Ambassador to India, John Kenneth Galbraith, has remarked, this is "without question . . . the most important and humane task on which men are now engaged." [6]

THREE KEY ISSUES

But how can an underdeveloped country go about achieving these vital objectives? How can it overcome the numerous obstacles we have mentioned? In the next chapter we shall discuss two important and widely

[6] John Kenneth Galbraith, *Economic Development in Perspective* (Cambridge: Harvard University Press, 1962), p. vi.

different approaches—those of India and China—to these difficult questions. Here, let us simply sketch out three pivotal issues which virtually all underdeveloped countries must face. These are: (1) the attempt to raise the rate of capital formation; (2) the question of "balance" between agriculture and industry; and (3) the problem of coping with population growth.

Raising the Rate of Investment

One of the most important tasks facing an underdeveloped country in its efforts to achieve economic progress will be raising the rate of investment or capital formation. These countries are, without exception, capital-poor. Moreover, since advanced technologies often require large amounts of capital, the rate of investment will typically place a limit on the degree of technological progress which such countries can achieve.[7]

The difficulties of raising the rate of investment in a very poor country are fairly obvious. Since investment typically takes resources which could have been used for consumption, the present burden of accumulating capital is a painful and, beyond a certain point, intolerable one. Moreover, this burden may be felt not only in terms of *discomfort* but in terms of present and future *productivity* as well. If workers do not receive enough to eat, they may work less efficiently, and the productive span of their working lives may be shortened; they may also lose the incentive to put forth their best efforts. In other words, if the lid is put on *too* tight—that is, if consumption is always kept to the bare minimum—then much of the steam may go out of the growth process in general, or, at least, it may have to be supplied by force and coercion.

There are, then, certain fundamental limits beyond which further attempts to raise the rate of investment might actually be self-defeating. Within these limits, there are, of course, many different ways in which a country can go about mobilizing additional investment. No one of these ways is "best" but all have certain specific advantages and disadvantages and, in practice, virtually all methods will be used at once.

If the economy is a "labor surplus" economy, investment may be increased as laborers are absorbed at low wages into the industrial sphere, permitting industrial profits and reinvestment of earnings. Economists have also suggested the use of unemployed or disguised unemployed laborers in various rural capital and construction projects—building roads, irrigation

---

[7] It is important to remember here that investment includes investment not only in tangible capital but in *intangible* capital as well. The importance of education and technical training to the modern underdeveloped country has been greatly stressed in recent economic literature and it probably cannot be stressed too much. To quote Galbraith again: "Literate people will see the need for getting machines. It is not so clear that machines will see the need for literate people. So under some circumstances at least popular education will have a priority over dams, factories, and other furniture of capital development." (*Ibid.*, pp. 8-9.) The task of raising the rate of investment, therefore, should be thought of as providing resources for *both* kinds of capital.

ditches, dams, and the like. The advantage of such methods is that they make use, at small cost, of resources that would otherwise be idle. The disadvantage is that these methods are difficult to apply. If agricultural production is inadequate, then the supply of cheap labor for the industrial sector may be checked off. Furthermore, rural workers are hard to mobilize; they require tools and managers, both of which may be in short supply; agricultural production may fall when this labor is withdrawn unless there is a reorganization of the agricultural system; and so on. In sum, the potential is there, but it is by no means easy to tap it.

And this is generally the case with the various methods by which an underdeveloped country may try to raise its investment rate. Take the matter of increased *taxation*. By *taxation,* the government takes away part of the country's resources and either makes them available to private investors or engages in capital construction projects of its own. Russia, for a long time, has financed much of her capital formation through a heavy "turn-over" tax. In early Japanese development, a substantial land-tax provided the resources for important investment undertakings. In almost all underdeveloped countries, some attempt must be made to raise the general level of tax collections if investment is to be increased.

Taxation also has its limits and difficulties, however. Taxes may have adverse effects on incentives. Taxes on the poor are limited by the depths of already existing poverty. Taxes on the rich, on the other hand, may deplete potential sources of saving, may penalize economic success and—if the rich happen to be in political power—may be difficult to enact in the first place. Moreover, in predominantly agricultural communities, taxes may be exceedingly hard to collect. Farmers are notoriously difficult to tax and, in the underdeveloped countries, where a great deal of production does not even come to a market, the problem is likely to be very serious indeed. Thus, while an increase in taxes can be regarded as a virtual necessity for most underdeveloped countries, the obstacles to its effective realization cannot be overlooked.

So it is also with a third method of capital accumulation. Faced with the difficulties of taxation, the government of an underdeveloped country may simply decide to increase its investment spending *without* increasing taxes. In this case, *inflation* becomes the mechanism for capital formation. Spending increases, prices rise, the consumer's dollar (or more likely, peso or rupee) declines in real value, and the physical consumption of the community is curtailed. This method has the virtue not only of being easy to apply but also of providing a stimulus to private investment. Prices are rising, profits are generally high, the economy is moving upward—isn't this the right time to expand plant and equipment? Indeed, the majority of economists would probably agree with the notion that "a little inflation may be a good thing" in a country attempting to achieve development.

The trouble with a "little" inflation is that it may turn into a "big" one. **93** This has been a perpetual problem in Latin America. In Chile, in the early fifties, price increases were occurring at the rate of 60 per cent to 80 per cent per year. In Bolivia, the cost-of-living index rose 25 times from 1953 to 1958. Brazil's price level rose between 5 and 6 times between 1958 and 1963. And a "big" inflation *does* have serious consequences. It may distort the pattern of capital formation and turn it into speculative channels. It may also give rise to serious international balance-of-payments problems. A country undergoing a major inflation may find that it is losing its foreign markets and thus the wherewithal to import the industrial products and capital goods necessary to its development efforts. The danger of a cumulative upward spiral of wages and prices thus makes *inflation* a limited, and always slightly perilous, method of capital accumulation.

In each case, then, we find certain advantages but also definite limits to any given method of raising the rate of investment. In most countries, the over-all result is likely to be that all methods together still produce an insufficient achievement. Taxes are hard to raise, the unemployed are difficult to mobilize, inflation runs the danger of becoming chronic. Even with the best of wills, the country will find that the gap between what seems necessary and what has been accomplished remains a large one.

It is here, of course, that the role of *foreign aid* in assisting underdeveloped countries becomes such a critical one. Needless to say, even *foreign aid* is no panacea. If the provision of capital from abroad simply becomes a substitute for domestic effort, then no net gain will have been achieved. Moreover, there are countless political difficulties which complicate the picture, not only for the giving but for the receiving country as well. Nevertheless, it is difficult to see how most underdeveloped countries will be able to meet their enormous investment needs without at least some substantial assistance from abroad. Lacking such assistance, their development efforts will almost certainly proceed at a much slower pace. Or—as is all too likely—they may decide to try to *force* a high rate of growth by turning to the harsh, but sometimes effective, methods of the totalitarian state.

Balanced Growth: Agriculture vs. Industry

A second key problem for an underdeveloped country concerns the "balance" to be preserved between the different sectors of its economy. Should special attention be given to industry? to agriculture? Should the country attempt to achieve a generally *balanced growth* in which both industry and agriculture develop side by side? How should the priorities be determined?

These are among the most important and deeply debated issues facing modern underdeveloped countries. The truth is that past experience gives no certain guide to the answer. It can probably be argued that, in most of the developed countries of the world, both industrial and agricultural improvements went hand in hand. This was certainly true of the United States; it was also true of England, where both prior and contemporaneous improvements in agriculture did much to make the revolution in the industrial sector possible. On the other hand, there is the example of the Soviet Union with its constant emphasis on heavy industry and—at least until very recently— its equally constant neglect of farm production. And yet the U.S.S.R., too, managed to achieve a very rapid increase in its output per capita.

There are, indeed, strong arguments on each side. Those who favor giving a special priority to industry and letting agriculture fend for itself might say something like the following:

> An underdeveloped country has only limited resources to give to investment and growth. Under these circumstances, it simply cannot do everything at once; it must choose those areas which promise the greatest development. And what are those areas? Clearly not agriculture, but industry. Indeed, modern growth and industrialization are really synonymous phenomena. Even in countries like New Zealand and Denmark, which have made a specialty of agricultural exports, the percentage of the labor force in industry is much higher than in most underdeveloped countries. Furthermore, the notion that an underdeveloped country should develop its agricultural sector and then export primary products in exchange for industrial products is a specious one. There is a long-run trend for the prices of primary products to fall relative to the prices of industrial and manufactured goods. This means that the prices that the poor country would have to pay would be constantly rising. No, much better to develop a strong industrial sector *within* the country! Instead of spreading her efforts thin, the country must concentrate her all on this critical task. In time, these efforts will produce a nucleus of skilled, energetic, growth-minded people and, through them, a spark will be kindled which will ignite the rest of the population.

In opposition to this, those who favor a more balanced approach in which agriculture and industry develop in a complementary relationship might say:

> It is useless to talk about developing industry and not agriculture because it will not work. Industry is dependent on agriculture for the raw materials and other inputs which make production possible. Moreover, as the economy develops, the population will demand more food. If you try rapid industrialization without adequate attention to agriculture, you will find yourself in a situation—as happened in certain industries in Yugoslavia —where industrial capacity is standing idle because of the lack of the necessary inputs. Or perhaps it will be like Argentina which ruined its agriculture through a massive industrialization effort and ended up one year actually having to import wheat from the United States. In general, the expansion of industry will call for an increase in the production of agricultural products, and if these demands are not met, there will be rising agricultural prices, heavy imports and—very probably—a real crisis in the country's international balance of payments. Furthermore, agriculture has a positive *advantage* as against industry in that small doses of scarce capital often bring far greater returns in agriculture than they do in the more capital-intensive industrial sector. Finally, don't worry about the problem of the prices of industrial imports rising relative to the prices of primary product exports. There is no evidence of a clear long-run trend in this

direction, and in the case of some primary products the future prospects look very rosy.[8]

This debate about agriculture vs. industry is really part of a more general argument over whether an underdeveloped country should try to achieve progress in a variety of different directions simultaneously or whether it should focus its efforts dramatically on certain key or "leading" sectors of the economy. In a certain sense, both points of view derive from a recognition of the same fact: namely, that there is significant interdependence between the different sectors of an economy. The *balanced growth* advocates proceed from this fact to the conclusion that the country must achieve advances simultaneously over a broad range of activities: Given interdependence, any isolated effort is likely to fail. The critics of this thesis, however, proceeding from the same fact, reach exactly the opposite conclusion. Thus, for example, Professor A. O. Hirschman, in a provocative book,[9] argues that the linkages between different industries provide a good reason for concentrating on certain specific areas of the economy only. By building up one stage or sector of industry, the country will set up heavy demands for productive increases in the lagging parts. While the *balanced growth* theorists try to *ease* tensions by establishing a harmonious, over-all pattern of development, Hirschman urges the *creation* of tensions between different parts of the economy so that the pressure for increased production calls forth a response.

At the present moment, these matters remain unsettled, and the debate will probably continue for many years to come. One important point which does emerge from the debate, however, is a clear recognition of the great

[8] The student should notice that part of the disagreement between these opposing viewpoints concerns differences of opinion about the future international markets for (1) primary and agricultural products as opposed to (2) industrial and manufactured products. This has been a hotly debated question in the development field during the past few years. Some economists have argued that past trends and future prospects alike indicate a deterioration in the "terms of trade" (the ratio of the prices a country receives for its exports to the prices it pays for its imports) of the primary-producing countries. The leading exponent of this view is Argentina's Dr. Raoul Prebisch, adviser to the United Nations' Economic Commission for Latin America; and, in fact, this argument is often referred to as the "Prebisch thesis." Other economists contend that the evidence presented for a continuing deterioration in the "terms of trade" is insufficient and that vast differences between particular commodities make such generalizations misleading. For some of the arguments on these questions, the student should see Raoul Prebisch, "The Role of Commercial Policies in Underdeveloped Countries," *American Economic Review Papers and Proceedings,* XLIV (May, 1959); Robert F. Gemmill, "Prebisch on Commercial Policy for Less-Developed Countries," *The Review of Economics and Statistics,* XLIV (May, 1962); Gottfried Haberler, *International Trade and Economic Development* (Cairo: National Bank of Egypt, 1959); Theodore W. Schultz, "Economic Prospects of Primary Products," *Economic Development for Latin America* (Proceedings of a conference held by the International Economic Association. London: Macmillan, 1961); Bela Balassa, *Trade Prospects for Developing Countries* (Homewood, Ill.: Irwin, 1964).

[9] Albert O. Hirschman, *The Strategy of Economic Development* (New Haven: Yale University Press, 1958). For a general statement of the *balanced growth* position, see Nurkse, *op. cit.*

interdependence between the different sectors of a country's economy. Industrial development necessarily places heavy demands on the agricultural sector. If an economy tries to develop its industry exclusively it will almost certainly create great strains in the domestic economy, and also internationally, because of its need for increased imports. This is not to say that an industrial orientation is misguided—some would claim that this is the *only* way development can be achieved. But it does suggest that such an "unbalanced" approach may require quite stringent controls over the general economic life of the country if it is not to lead to severe crises.

Population Policy

Our third key issue concerns the means available for coping with the population problem. This problem is, of course, particularly severe in the populous countries of Asia, but in the sense that a high rate of population growth is typical throughout the underdeveloped world it has a bearing on the future prospects of all poor countries.

Fundamentally, there are two ways of approaching the problem of population growth. The first is to take the rate of population growth as given and to try to cope with its effects. The other is to try to alter the rate of increase itself.

If the first approach is used exclusively, it is usually because various religious or ideological reasons make any general attempt to curb human population repugnant to those in power. In such cases, the efforts of the country are necessarily directed toward effects rather than causes and, in particular, to the common problem of growing unemployment. The industrial capital stock is not growing rapidly enough to employ such massive increases in the labor force, and the land—at least in the more heavily populated countries—cannot effectively employ them either. Under these circumstances *employment-creation* becomes an independent goal of national policy. The mobilization of the rural unemployed in community development projects where village authorities cooperate with the government in undertaking local public-works programs becomes a task of high priority. The country, furthermore, may attempt to emphasize high-labor/low-capital industries. Thus, a handicraft industry may be preferred to its factory equivalent, not on the grounds of efficiency, but because it provides more jobs for those who would otherwise go idle. The difficulty here, of course, is that the goals of employment-creation and economic growth do not invariably coincide. Should a country use its scarce capital where it will provide the most jobs or where it will provide the greatest increase in output? Since no social and political system could survive an indefinite increase in unemployment, this problem will sometimes cause a departure from the objective of the fastest possible rate of growth.

The second approach concerns itself with the attempt to *lower* the rate **97** of population increase, usually through various campaigns for family planning which are designed to reduce the birth-rate.[10] Our own value judgments aside, there do not seem to be any fundamental religious or ideological obstacles to making such attempts in the more populous underdeveloped countries. Hinduism, for example, appears to be tolerant of such attempts and has even been interpreted by some partisans as favoring them. Communist China represents a rather special situation, which we will discuss in the next chapter, but even here birth control has come back into favor in recent years. In this sense, then, such programs do represent a practical possibility and, in fact, many countries are now attempting to carry them out.

At the same time, however, experience suggests that programs of this nature may be a long time in having any major effect on the rates of population growth in most of these countries. The problems of lack of education, of expense, of inadequate or unsuitable methods, and, more deeply, of the absence of those general social attitudes toward having fewer children which seem to come primarily as a *result* of industrialization—all these difficulties suggest that even those countries which go all-out in their attempts to reduce the birth-rate will find that results come slowly. The one Asiatic country which has made definite strides in this direction is Japan which, in great part due to the use of legalized abortion, has substantially lowered its birth-rate in recent years. Japan, however, is at a higher stage of urban and industrial development than its Asiatic neighbors and, therefore, it is doubtful that her experience can be generalized to cover their problems.

The conclusion, therefore, is that even those countries most committed to this second approach will probably also find themselves coping with the effects of a too-rapid rate of population increase for many years to come. This, of course, is not necessarily an argument for abandoning programs designed to stem the population tide. Indeed, some would say that it is an argument for stepping them up to the maximum degree feasible.

SUMMARY

Over the past century or more, the gap between the rich and the poor countries of the world has been constantly widening. In Asia, Africa, and much of Latin America the central economic problem remains one of breaking through a centuries'-old pattern of stagnation. Poverty in these areas is often extreme, with levels of annual output per capita of $100 and less characterizing perhaps half the world's population. Over-all, two-thirds of the world can be said to be living in seriously underdeveloped areas.

Poverty in these areas is not new but the determination to overcome

[10] There is, of course, the *theoretical* possibility of also working at the other end of the scale: i.e., raising the death-rate, or, what it would actually come down to, reducing efforts to improve public health and other conditions which might, if effected, bring a further decline in the death-rate. Apart from the obvious moral reservations one might feel, it is at least doubtful whether such a policy would be effective.

it is. This determination, largely a product of contact with the West, is the real driving force behind all attempts at "getting started" in these countries. Unfortunately, however, these attempts face very serious obstacles. Despite the advantage of a ready-made industrial technology which can be "borrowed" from the economically advanced countries, the modern underdeveloped country often has to cope with much more difficult problems than did its nineteenth-century predecessors. For one thing, the available technology, with its heavy demands on capital and trained personnel, is by no means ideally suited to conditions in underdeveloped countries, where these items are scarce and untrained labor is abundant. For another, these countries lack the social and economic preparation of their predecessors and thus must attempt to accomplish not one but several revolutions at the same time. To make matters still worse, the modern underdeveloped country—particularly in Asia—faces extremely acute population problems. A "public-health revolution" has made rapid rates of population increase common throughout the underdeveloped world, and many of these countries are already densely populated in relation to their resources. And, finally, the poor climate for private foreign investment means that the gap to be filled by foreign governmental assistance in these countries is a very substantial one.

Given these obstacles and the simple arithmetic of the situation, it is doubtful whether any of the modern underdeveloped countries can hope to "catch up" to or even seriously narrow the gap which separates them from countries like the United States over the course of the next century. What they can hope to do, however, is to remove the extremes of poverty which limit the possibilities of a normal human existence. The attempt to accomplish this important goal will typically involve these countries in three key problems:

1. How to raise the rate of investment? The mobilization of unemployed workers, increases in taxes, and inflation are all means by which a country may hope to raise its investment rate. Each method has its own special advantages and difficulties, and it is likely that most countries will use all in one degree or another. Even then, it is probable that the sum total will be insufficient without foreign aid or, alternatively, the use of coercive methods.

2. What kind of "balance" to seek between the industrial and agricultural sectors of the economy? Should industry be given the first priority or should an attempt be made to ease the strains of development by trying to improve agriculture simultaneously? Experience gives no certain guide in this matter although it does seem clear that exclusive attention to industry will necessarily require a fairly tight control over the economy as a whole.

3. How to cope with the effects and causes of rising population? An underdeveloped country may try to make use of its growing numbers by emphasizing highly labor-intensive projects and may also try to stem the growing tide by family-planning campaigns. In either case, it seems likely **99** that the population problem will be a serious one in these countries for many decades to come.

Alternative Approaches

—India and China

CHAPTER SIX

Of all the economic revolutions now in progress in the underdeveloped world, none is of greater interest than those taking place in India and in mainland China. India and China comprise roughly a third of the world's population. Their indirect influence extends throughout Asia and to poor countries everywhere. Both countries have experienced staggering poverty in the midst of twentieth-century affluence; both have awakened to the need for economic development; both have instituted governmental planning to achieve this end. But here the resemblance stops. In India economic planning is being undertaken by a democratically elected state in a context of mixed public and private enterprise. In China an authoritarian state has attempted to direct, control, and regiment every conceivable aspect of economic life. For the student of economic development—and, indeed, for all men everywhere—these two countries offer a fascinating study in the mechanisms for initiating modern growth.

SIMILARITY
OF THE BASIC PROBLEMS

Although different in many particulars, the problems of achieving a breakthrough in India and in China show a number of important similarities. They are both large and populous countries. India's area is about two-fifths that of the United States and her population in 1965 was roughly 480 million. China's area is approximately equal to that of the United States and her population in 1965 was of the order of 750 million. In both countries population has been increasing, in India at a current rate of around 2½ per cent per year and in China at slightly over 2 per cent per year. Recent estimates have it that India's population in 1976 will be 625 million. Not long after that, China may reach the 1 billion mark.

There are also important parallels in the past histories of these countries. Both have been the centers of great civilizations and both have been under the domination of the West throughout much of the nineteenth and twentieth centuries. In India this domination took the form of explicit British rule until the Indian Independence Act of 1947. China was nominally independent, but, after being opened to Western trade by the Treaty of Nanking in 1842, she was subjected to a series of treaties and special concessions to foreigners which, taken together, placed her in a kind of semi-colonial status. In each country, furthermore, a new regime took over in the post-World War II period and in conditions which were far from auspicious. India faced the enormous problems involved in the partition of India and Pakistan. China, fresh from civil war, plunged recklessly into Korea.

From an economic point of view, India and China in the immediate post-war period were at approximately the same stage of development, or rather, lack of development. They were both overwhelmingly rural, capital-poor, technologically primitive economies with very low levels of output per capita. A reasonable guess would be that the two countries were at that time on a roughly equal footing—India having a slight advantage in industry, China, in agriculture—and that annual per-capita output in each case ran in the neighborhood of $80 to $120. This, of course, was an extremely low standard.[1]

Finally, as we would expect, both countries were faced with enormous social and political as well as purely economic problems. In China the traditional orientation of the society toward the family and the lack of an effective central government had long made reforms of any kind difficult to carry out. For her part, India had her castes, her multiplicity of languages, and her ancient religious traditions from which even her modern constitution could not altogether escape.[2] In short, the problem in neither country has

---

[1] For a discussion of some of the measurement problems, particularly for China, see Alexander Eckstein, *The National Income of Communist China* (Glencoe, Ill.: The Free Press, 1961), pp. 65-69.

[2] The most notable example being the problem of the sacred cow. Thus, the modern Indian constitution states: "The State shall endeavor to organize agriculture and animal husbandry on modern and scientific lines and shall in particular, take steps for preserving and improving the breeds, and prohibiting the slaughter of cows and calves and other milch and draught cattle." To a Western observer, this statement must seem a contradiction in terms. It indicates the kind of social and cultural problem countries like India face in attempting economic development.

been one of an industrial revolution alone; it has involved little less than the attempt to re-make the entire social order.

CONTRASTING METHODS

If their problems have shown many similarities, the methods of approaching them in India and China have often been in sharp contrast. One such contrast has to do with the tempo of their development programs. Although she has not escaped significant readjustments in her approach, China has basically proceeded on a forced-draft basis. "Twenty years compressed into one day," the "great leap forward," the goal of overtaking Great Britain in the production of electric power and other industrial goods within a decade—such slogans and objectives convey a sense of the seriousness and urgency with which the Chinese have approached their task. India has been no less serious, but she has perhaps been rather less urgent. She too has had to readjust her goals to uncomfortable realities, but the goals have at least always been rationally arrived at. In contrast to China, India's approach seems much more "gradualistic."

This difference, in turn, is at least partly a reflection of the Indian emphasis on voluntarism as opposed to compulsion and of the quite different role of the central government in the two countries. Government planning has, of course, played a key role in India's development effort. This effort began in earnest with the launching of a Five Year Plan in 1951; subsequently, there has been a Second Plan (1956-1961), a Third Plan (1961-1966), and beginning in 1967, having been postponed for a year, a projected Fourth Plan (1967-1972). Moreover, it is also true that India's efforts have been directed not only toward growth in the narrow sense but toward the creation of what is called a "socialistic pattern of society." Such a society, according to the Second Five Year Plan report, means "that the basic criterion for determining the lines of advance must not be private profit but social gain, and that the pattern of development and the structure of socio-economic relations should be so planned that they result not only in appreciable increases in national income and employment but also in greater equality in income and wealth." [3] India thus conceives herself as moving toward her own particular native brand of socialism.

Such statements, however, should not be confused with the situation as it actually exists in India at the present time. In many respects the Indian government plays a smaller role in her economy than do the governments of the so-called "mixed" economies of the Western world. India's total tax collections, for example, are a much smaller percentage of her national income than those of the United States. Her ratio of government expenditures to

102

[3] Government of India Planning Commission, Second Five Year Plan (1956), Ch. 2, p. 22.

total expenditures is among the lowest in the world. It should be remembered, furthermore, that India is primarily an agricultural economy and that her emphasis in the agricultural sphere has been on voluntary community development programs (as opposed, for example, to compulsory collectivization or state ownership). In other words, the Indian economy has preserved a very large private sector and the role of the government, while increasing, is by no means without definite limits.[4]

In this respect, the contrast with China is sharp and clear. In China we have an illustration of the emergence of a modern totalitarian state in conditions of extreme economic backwardness. Despite the inherent difficulties of controlling such a large, agrarian economy, the Chinese communist government moved forward rapidly until, by the late 1950's, it was attempting to dominate virtually every aspect of the country's life. In industry, for example, by 1956-1957—less than a decade after the communists came to power— governmental investment was 96.7 per cent of all industrial investment.[5] In agriculture a succession of steps quickly prepared the way for the regimentation of the rural labor force. First, there was the process of land reform which eliminated (often by death) the former land-owners and caused the land to be redistributed to the peasants. Then, the land was taken away from the peasants again through collectivization. By the end of 1956, 87 per cent of all farm households were organized in "producers' cooperatives of the advanced type." Then, in 1958, came the "great leap forward" and the famous *communes* under which even the small private plots of ground formerly reserved for family use were collectivized and the whole of agricultural and rural-industrial production was brought under almost military control. In 1960, the retreat from the "great leap forward" was accompanied by the

---

[4] India's over-all approach to the problem of balance between the public and private sectors of the economy was set out in her Industrial Policy Resolution of 1956. Here she divided industries into three groups: (1) industries the development of which will be the exclusive responsibility of the state (e.g., arms and munitions, atomic energy, iron and steel, heavy electrical plant, coal, mineral oils, iron-mining, air and railway transport, shipbuilding, telephones, electricity, etc.); (2) industries which will be progressively state-owned; the state will take the initiative in establishing new enterprises but private enterprise will supplement state efforts (e.g., other minerals, machine tools, nonferrous metals, fertilizers, road transport, sea transport, etc.); and (3) industries the future development of which will be left to private initiative (all other industries). This resolution, if eventually carried out, would, of course, put the state in a commanding position over most of the vital areas of Indian industry. But again it should be pointed out that this is a statement of objectives rather than of facts; private enterprises now exist even in the first sector (the exclusively state sector) and will presumably continue to do so for some time to come. All this is not to deny, however, that state intervention in the Indian economy has, in some respects, been a disadvantage to private economic initiative. Some observers feel that the economy would have made greater progress during the past decade if private enterprise had been given more active encouragement.

[5] By this time (1956-1957), in fact, there were virtually no purely private industrial enterprises left in China. The government had become either a co-owner or a stockholder along with private parties and was even organizing traders and peddlers into cooperatives.

relaxation of many of the more stringent features of the communes. Trade fairs were reintroduced and the government encouraged the restoration of small private garden plots. By 1963, control of agriculture had been shifted from the commune to the much smaller production team. But this retreat gives no evidence of being anything but a temporary adjustment to realities; there is still a possibility of further thoroughgoing socialist reforms of agriculture.

Furthermore, as the above suggests, the Chinese state has been the driving force behind the *social* revolution which has been accompanying the economic. In India, too, the government has attempted important social reforms, as, for example, in its effort to abolish ancient caste distinctions and to improve the lot of the "untouchables." But the actions of the Chinese government have unquestionably been far more drastic and far-reaching in this area. Some of these actions, like the passage of the Marriage Law of 1950 which prohibits parental interference in marriage choices or the buying of brides, would probably meet the approval of most Western observers. Others, such as the massive increase in loudspeaker propaganda or the attempt to elevate loyalty to the state above that to the family, strike a note reminiscent of George Orwell's *1984*. The story of the woman who reports her politically errant husband to the authorities and gets elected "anti-bandit hero, special class," may be a fine example of patriotism rewarded; but it hardly suggests much sensitivity to individual human relationships. In 1966, the great "cultural revolution" under the aegis of the fanatic "Red Guards" seems to outdo Orwell. Value judgments aside, however, the important point is that the Chinese communist government has made in the social as well as in the economic sphere a much more pronounced effort to control and direct the course of change than has its Indian counterpart.

Let us now see how these differences in methods are reflected in the two countries' responses to the "key" issues outlined in the last chapter.

RAISING
THE RATE OF INVESTMENT

In both India and China there have been definite efforts to raise the rate of investment but with quite different results. It should be pointed out that the difficulties of accurately comparing investment and production in these two countries are very great and, in the last few years, owing to the paucity of Chinese statistics, really insurmountable. Even given such difficulties, however, the fundamental differences of approach are very evident.

India

104   The Government of India estimates that net investment rose from around 5 per cent of national income at the beginning of the First Five Year

Plan (1951) to about 8 per cent at the beginning of the Second Plan (1956), and then to roughly 11 per cent at the beginning of the Third (1961). By 1965/1966, estimated investment was running at about 14 per cent of national income.

On the face of it, these figures would seem to suggest a fairly substantial improvement in India's rate of capital formation. When we examine the matter more closely, however, we find that the rate of progress is slightly less than one might have inferred. Although India has attempted to use all the various devices available for accumulating more capital, each has proved to have its own special difficulties. Despite her great reservoirs of unemployed or quasi-unemployed laborers, she has found it impossible to utilize this resource for effective large-scale capital formation. She has come to regard inflationary methods with great caution because of a balance-of-payments crisis that developed in the middle of the Second Plan period. Taxes have gone up, but it is hard to raise taxes substantially in a poor, agrarian, and democratic country, and, furthermore, non-developmental needs have also been increasing. In the early 1960's, as a result of the Chinese border violations, Indian military expenditures increased from $800 million to $2.8 billion. And, in 1965, of course, there was the sharp confrontation between India and Pakistan which meant further demands on governmental revenues.

Table 6-1 GROSS AID RECEIVED BY INDIA FROM ALL SOURCES

Year	Total Aid (millions of dollars)	Per-Capita Aid (dollars)
1961/62	712	1.63
1962/63	941	2.09
1963/64	1,235	2.68
1964/65 (est)	1,500	3.18

Source: Edward S. Mason, "Economic Development in India and Pakistan," Harvard University Center for International Affairs, Occasional Paper, No. 13, September, 1966, p. 20.

The consequence of all this is that while domestic savings have risen in India—in 1964-1965 they were perhaps 11 to 12 per cent of GNP—she has not been able to finance her developmental effort except with substantial foreign assistance. From 1961 to 1965, total foreign aid to India, including agricultural assistance under P. L. 480, more than doubled and per-capita aid almost doubled. During the course of the Second Plan, foreign aid probably accounted for about 14 per cent of India's gross investment; by 1965, it was accounting for as much as 25 per cent of her gross investment. This is not to say that India has been receiving excessive aid. Indeed, there are other countries that have been receiving more on a per capita basis.[6] Furthermore,

[6] On a per capita basis, Pakistan, for example, has been receiving almost twice the aid India has been receiving. See Mason, *op. cit.*, pp. 20-21.

India's need for foreign assistance derives not simply from her need to increase investment but also because her development effort requires significant imports from abroad. Without aid, she would undoubtedly have faced even more serious balance-of-payments crises than she already has faced. Still, it remains true that foreign assistance has provided a substantial and growing fraction of India's developmental investment and this despite three major Five Year Plans aimed at achieving at least the beginnings of self-sustaining growth.

China

China's experience has been substantially different from that of India. Although the data are incomplete and unsatisfactory, it seems clear that China has raised her rate of investment faster and maintained it at a higher level than that of India. One comparison with respect to *gross* investment [7] as a percentage of gross national product shows India increasing her gross investment from 9.3 per cent in 1950 to 13.6 per cent in 1957. During the same period, it is estimated that China increased her gross investment from 9.7 per cent in 1950 (roughly the same as India) to 23.9 per cent in 1957 (or about 75 per cent more than that of India.) [8] A recent estimate puts China's gross investment in 1959 at 25.7 per cent of gross national product,[9] a very high level for a seriously underdeveloped country such as China is.

This achievement was bought only at the cost of a great strain on the Chinese economy, all the more so since it was accomplished largely through domestic as opposed to foreign sources. Russian aid was critical at a certain point in Chinese development, but, as far as the specific task of capital formation is concerned, it played a secondary role. There have been no known Russian financial grants to China. Even Russian loans were on a comparatively small scale, covering only a fraction of China's public investment during her first Five Year Plan (1953-1957). Where Russian assistance was indispensable was in the area of technical aid (providing engineers, blueprints, helping in the installation of new plants, training personnel) and in serving as a source of trade whereby China could import her needed capital goods in return for exports of agricultural and mineral products. With the great rift between Russia and China in the 1960's, even this kind of assistance has disappeared. Russian technicians were withdrawn in 1960; China has had to repay such credits as she received from the U.S.S.R.; trade between the

---

[7] Gross investment here includes replacement investment and also an allowance for investment made in rural areas on a non-financial or barter basis.

[8] Wilfred Malenbaum, "India and China: Contrasts in Development," *American Economic Review,* Vol. XLIX (June, 1959).

[9] William W. Hollister, "Capital Function in Communist China," in Choh-Ming Li, ed., *Industrial Development in Communist China* (New York: Praeger, 1964). It is Hollister's opinion that in the period 1958 through 1960, China was actually "over-investing"—i.e., that she was adding more to her capital stock than the economy could absorb and consequently was wasting important economic resources.

two countries has been on the decline. What this means is that the basic sacrifice of present to future has been China's own.

The state, of course, has been the overwhelmingly dominant factor in China's effort to raise her investment rate. Increased investment has been made possible largely by compulsory collective savings in the form of taxes, the profits and depreciation reserves of state-controlled enterprises, and the reserve funds of farm units. From 1950 to 1952, tax receipts more than doubled and they continued to increase substantially throughout that decade. Furthermore, there were strong efforts to mobilize rural labor and squeeze savings and investment out of the agricultural sector. The communes in particular appear to have had as a primary aim the organization of rural labor resources with the idea of setting them to work not only on agricultural improvements but also on industrial projects such as the famous "backyard blast furnaces" for increasing iron and steel production. In general, China appears to have worked much more intensively at the task of extracting a surplus from the agricultural sector than has India and in this way has attempted to broaden her base for domestic capital formation. The difficulties of such efforts, however, have also become clear. The "backyard blast furnaces" had to be given up because they produced an inadequate product; the strains put on agriculture have led to great disorganization and to the consequent abandonment of the essential features of the communes. Also, since rural poverty is as pervasive a phenomenon in China as it is in India, the attempt to raise the investment rate has been bought only at a deep human cost.

AGRICULTURE VS. INDUSTRY

In the beginning, China did not hesitate to sacrifice agriculture to industry at every turn, but she soon discovered that this was an unworkable policy. India has been somewhat more tentative and experimental, but she too has been discovering the need for greater attention to the agricultural sector.

India

The changing character of the "balance" of Indian developmental efforts is roughly suggested by the distribution of successive Plan outlays presented in Table 6-2. Perhaps the most notable shift is that which took place between the First Plan and the Second. Public outlays on industry and minerals rose from 4 per cent in the First Plan to 20 per cent in the Second. At the same time, the area of agriculture and community development declined from 15 per cent to 11 per cent, irrigation from 16 per cent to 9 per cent and power from 13 per cent to 10 percent. There was, in short, a substantial shift in the direction of industry as opposed to agriculture. Indian planners had decided

Table 6-2 INDIA: PERCENTAGE DISTRIBUTION OF
PLAN OUTLAYS IN THE PUBLIC SECTOR

	1st Plan (1951-1956)	2nd Plan (1956-1961)	3rd Plan (Est: 1961-1966)
Agriculture and community development	15%	11%	14%
Irrigation	16%	9%	9%
Power	13%	10%	13%
Village and small industries	2%	4%	4%
Industry and minerals	4%	20%	20%
Transport and communications	27%	28%	20%
Social services and miscellaneous	23%	18%	20%
Total	100%	100%	100%

Source: Third Five Year Plan, p. 59.

at the beginning of the Second Plan that the time was now ripe for a major push in the direction of industrial development.

Unfortunately, it cannot be said that everything worked out quite as well as anticipated. During the period of the First Plan, two highly favorable monsoons had helped produce very substantial increases in agricultural production. During the Second Plan, however, the reverse happened: There was unfavorable weather, and food imports, which had been anticipated at 6 million tons, were, in fact, about 20 million tons during the 1956-1961 period. The problem was further complicated by the fact that there were considerable underestimates of the import requirements of the industrialization plan. The net effect of these and other difficulties was an international balance of payments crisis which developed in the middle of the plan period and caused a downward revision of many of the desired production goals.

As a consequence of this experience, the Planning Commission partially reversed the balance in the Third Plan. They affirmed:

> Experience in the first two Plans, and especially in the Second, has shown that the rate of growth in agricultural production is one of the main limiting factors in the progress of the Indian economy . . . The critical tests for the Third Plan are two: (a) the extent to which the production of food and raw materials can be increased—what is needed is a striking advance rather than a varying performance; and (b) the energy and drive that are forthcoming for securing the substantial increases needed in export earnings.[10]

India's conclusion, in other words, was that "balanced growth" is necessary, particularly where the inadequacy of export earnings makes reliance on heavy imports from abroad impracticable.

Unfortunately, it cannot be said that agricultural progress during the Third Plan has lived up to Indian expectations. Food grain production was stagnant from the good year 1960-1961 (81 million tons) to 1963-1964

[10] Government of India, Third Five Year Plan (1961), pp. 49, 117.

(80.2 million tons). In 1964-1965, there was an excellent crop (88.4 million tons) but in 1965-1966, there was bad weather and food grain production fell below what it had been at the start of the planning period and very far below the originally scheduled target of 100 million tons. Fertilizer production and consumption were also disappointing, falling well below planned targets.[11] Had it not been for substantial food imports from the United States in 1966, it is possible that India would have suffered a major famine.

China

If the need for "balanced growth" in agriculture and industry has become apparent to Indian planners, the same lesson has been brought home to the Chinese and even more dramatically. China is also a country with a foreign exchange problem: her foreign exchange reserves are low and there is no foreign aid to assist her. Nevertheless, she tried at the beginning of her development effort to put the bulk of her resources in the industrial sector. Table 6-3 gives the distribution of planned investment expenditures under the Chinese First Five Year Plan (1953-1957). Although the actual allocation of investment to agriculture eventually exceeded the original figure,[12] the lack of "balance" for what is still a dominantly agrarian country is striking. Furthermore, within industry, the emphasis was on heavy, investment-goods producing industries rather than on light, consumers'-goods industries, so that "balance," as far as consumer demand is concerned, was even further ignored.

Table 6-3 CHINA: DISTRIBUTION OF INVESTMENT IN THE FIRST FIVE YEAR PLAN (1953-1957)

Sector	Billion Yuan	Percentage of Total
Industrial ministries	24.85	58.2%
Agriculture, forestry, and water conservancy	3.26	7.6
Transport, posts, and telephone communications	8.21	19.2
Trade, banking and stockpiling	1.28	3.0
Culture, education and public health	3.08	7.2
Development of municipal public utilities	1.60	3.7
Others	0.46	1.1

Source: China's First Five Year Plan, Peking, 1956.

Such a one-sided emphasis should have caused deep strains on the Chinese economy and there is reason to believe that it did. The year 1957 saw a general reduction in investment and production targets and a partial redress of the agricultural-industrial balance. But this was only partial and it

[11] See *Eastern Economist,* Annual Number 1966, p. 1267.

[12] In terms of realized state developmental investment, industry went down to 56 per cent and agriculture up to a little over 8 per cent during the 1953-1957 period. See Choh-Ming Li, "China," in Adamantios Pepelasis, Leo Mears and Irma Adelman, eds., *Economic Development* (New York: Harper, 1961), p. 372.

was also only temporary. The next year saw the coming of the "great leap forward," which meant a sharp rise in the goals for both agricultural and industrial production and an attempt simultaneously to retain the industrial emphasis of the central government's investment program and to step up agricultural production through the communes. In the year 1958, exclusive of internal investment in the communes, 65 per cent of all development investment was in industry, 13 per cent in transport and communication, and only 10 per cent in agriculture, forestry and water conservation. The Chinese thus held firm to their industrial goals (in fact, raised them) and tried to handle the agricultural problem by means of a much tighter and more disciplined organization of rural production.

That this approach was a costly failure now seems established beyond question. The great leap forward was not a carefully organized decentralization of the economy but "more like economic anarchy." [13] This, combined with poor weather, brought a series of bad harvests in 1959, 1960, and 1961. Even by 1963 grain production was probably still below the level achieved in 1957, the year before the "leap" began. The costs of this failure were felt not only in agriculture and in rural distress, but also in the industrial sector, which suffered a severe breakdown in the early 1960's, and in the international sphere, since China was forced to use precious reserves to import foreign grain. As a consequence of these developments, China has had to retreat from the unrealistic goals she set in the late 1950's and to increase the attention she is giving to the agricultural sector. Given the international aspirations of China, and her determination to become a dominant political and military power in Asia, however, it is not clear that she will hold back for long in her drive to become a major industrial nation.

POPULATION POLICY

Given China's general method of approach, one might have expected her to come up with a rather draconic "solution" to the population problem. In point of fact, however, China has shown a good deal of vacillation in this area while India has had a more consistent view of her objectives. In neither case can it be said that substantial progress has yet been achieved.

India

Population growth in India during the past dozen years has regularly exceeded the official projections and by a considerable amount. Thus, for example, the Second Five Year Plan was based on a projection of population growth which would have given India a population of 500 million in 1975-

[13] Dwight Perkins, *Market Control and Planning in Communist China* (Cambridge: Harvard University Press, 1966), p. 19.

1976. Five years later, as the provisional estimates from the 1961 Census became available, the drafters of the Third Five Year Plan estimated that population in 1976 would probably reach a total of 625 million. These great underestimates of population growth explain in part why the rate of growth in Indian output per capita has thus far been below expectation. They also help account for India's increasingly serious unemployment problem. There seems little doubt that the unemployment picture in India has "suffered significant deterioration" in recent years. At the end of the Second Plan (1961), it was conservatively estimated that there were 9 million unemployed workers in the Indian economy and another 15 to 18 million partially unemployed or underemployed workers. Since population growth has brought a further addition of 15 to 20 million workers to the labor force during the Third Five Year Plan period, the difficulties of the employment problem in this "labor surplus" economy are hard to overestimate.

Given this critical situation, India has necessarily had to make employment-creation one of the goals of her planning, as, for example, in her effort to protect handicraft workers in the textile industry against factory competition. She has also put increasing emphasis on family planning as a fundamental objective of her national policy. Thus, in the Third Plan, the government expressed the hope that family planning will become "a nationwide movement which embodies a basic attitude towards a better life for the individual, the family and the community."

As far as expenditure on family planning is concerned, the Indian government has been regularly increasing its allocations for this purpose. The funds allotted to the Family Planning Program have increased tenfold from the Second Plan to the Third (from a little over $10 million to a little over $100 million) and, although the Fourth Plan allocations are not yet available, it appears that there will be roughly a tripling of the Family Planning expenditure over the next five years.[14] At the same time, there has been major progress in the technology of birth control, especially through the development of the intra-uterine contraceptive device, known in India as "the loop." This device was tested in India and became available as a part of a state program in 1965. Six months later, 85,000 women had received loops in West Bengal state, 52,000 in Gugerat, 17,000 even in the small territory of Delhi. By early 1966, a factory established by the Indian government was producing 16,000 loops daily.

All this has given hope to those who see India's population growth as a major obstacle to her economic development. Still, progress so far in total has been very limited. There remains a shortage of trained personnel; India's 500,000 small villages are extremely difficult to reach in a national program; tradition and habit change only slowly. Consequently, although there is a

[14] See Government of India Planning Commission, *Fourth Five Year Plan—Resources, Outlays and Programs,* Twenty-second meeting of the National Development Council, September 5 and 6, 1965, p. 58.

definite promise in the future, the present rate of growth of India's population is still an alarming 2½ per cent per year.

China

While India has emphasized the desirability of limiting population growth almost from the beginning, China's policy has followed a curiously shifting and inconsistent course.

Broadly speaking, it can be said that, at the beginning of the communist regime, the official attitude was that population was an asset rather than a liability and that there was no need for any effort to control population increase. With the results of the first modern census of China becoming available in 1954 (showing a much larger population than had previously been imagined) and with a growing awareness of the rapidity of the rate of population increase, this attitude gradually altered and, by 1957, a national birth-control campaign was officially underway. But then, in 1958, the campaign was abruptly called off. According to Chairman Mao: "Our fast-expanding population is an objective fact and is our asset." [15] In the year of the "great leap forward," then, the official line reverted roughly to what it had been in the first period of the regime. Subsequently, it appears that this line has been in the process of erosion once again. Chinese newspapers have recently been pointing out the advantages of late marriages and the government has taken up the advocacy of birth-control measures. Thus there has been in effect a return to the family-planning objectives of the middle fifties.

Given our general lack of knowledge of what is going on in China, these shifts in population policy are by no means easy to account for. There are, however, certain factors which seem to have an important bearing on the matter. In the first place, Marxian theory is generally hostile to the notion of the existence of population problems. Karl Marx called Malthus's theory of population "a libel on the human race." The problem, according to Marx, was not population pressing against resources, but "capitalists" pressing against the "proletariat": i.e., it was the "system" that was at fault, not the natural laws of procreation or the limitations of resources. Secondly, the traditional Chinese religion makes the welfare of the dead in the after-life dependent on the sacrifices offered by their descendants; this means that any limitation on the number of children, and particularly sons, is hard medicine for many Chinese families to swallow. Thirdly, the acknowledgment of the existence of a population problem is, in effect, an acknowledgement that the state has not, after all, succeeded in its developmental goals. If communism can bring such phenomenal increases in production, then why this worry about the number of people to be fed and clothed?

Finally, and this may have particular bearing on the change in attitude at the time of the "great leap forward," population growth may be less of a liability if one is able to utilize effectively the increasing labor force. The

112

[15] Quoted by Richard Hughes, "China Makes a 'Bitter Retreat,'" *New York Times Magazine* (July 15, 1962), p. 36.

communes, on this interpretation, were China's (temporary) answer to the population problem: By establishing a rigorous organization and discipline in the countryside she attempted to make certain that the growing labor force would lead not to idleness and unemployment but to increasing production and capital formation. On this view, the difficulties with the communes and the retreat from the "great leap forward" mean that this answer had proved unworkable. China thus had no alternative except to return to her abandoned policy of trying to limit the rate of population growth.

All these points are necessarily somewhat conjectural. What is not conjectural is that China has not so far succeeded in stemming the tide of her growing numbers. Each year there are 14 or 15 million more Chinese; each year she comes closer to the magic (or tragic) number of 1 billion.

ACHIEVEMENTS AND COSTS

We have discussed some of the key differences between the developmental efforts of India and mainland China; the question now is— What have been the relative accomplishments and costs? What do the future prospects of these two countries appear to be?

The only completely reliable answer to such questions is: Time will tell. As we have said before, there is a staggering lack of accurate information on many, if not most, of the relevant aspects of the problem, particularly in the case of China. And this, of course, is apart from the problem of analyzing the significance of accurate figures if we had them.

One general conclusion to which virtually everyone can subscribe is that in each country the past 15 years have brought both accomplishments and a host of still unsolved problems. In India, the most important accomplishment has been an increase in the level of her total output and, more significantly, in the level of her output per capita. During the period 1950 to 1965, India's total output has been increasing at an annual percentage rate of between 3 and 4 per cent per year. Because of the unexpectedly rapid rate of population growth, the increase in output per capita has been less than had been hoped for but it did take place—at around 1 to 1½ per cent per year during this period. As such, it marked a definite improvement from the previous half century when Indian output per capita probably did not rise at all.

Against this improvement we must put India's many unsolved problems: Her progress in agriculture has been painfully slow. Her exports have grown much too slowly and she has become increasingly dependent on foreign assistance. She has barely scratched the surface of her population problem and her unemployment situation is serious. To add to her burdens in the 1960's is the rise in the level of her defense expenditures. This added charge **113** on her resources is a most serious matter when her rate of progress is already pitifully meager as against her acute needs. At her present pace, India would remain a very poor nation at the end of the century and many segments of her population would undoubtedly still be living in conditions of desperate poverty. Whether any social or political system could stand the strains of such prolonged misery, particularly after the mood of "rising expectations" had begun to take root, is an important and disturbing question.

In the case of China, there has also been an advance in the level of total output and output per capita, although in a much more uneven way. Until the debacle of the "great leap forward," the rate of advance almost certainly greatly exceeded that of India. This, of course, was particularly true of industrial output. In the period 1952 to 1957, some industrial sectors were growing at rates of 15 or even over 20 per cent per year. With the good harvest of 1958, agricultural production had also shown definite improvement. Thus, on the eve of the "great leap forward," China could boast an over-all rate of growth of national income that was not less than 4½ per cent and may have exceeded 6 per cent per year.[16]

Events subsequently, however, have shown that China also has her problems. To her credit, it can be said that she has apparently managed a satisfactory recovery from the crisis years of 1960 and 1961, and this despite the fact of the withdrawal of Russian technicians and the necessity of providing her investment effort purely from domestic sources. Nevertheless, the crisis was a severe one and it is not certain that she had re-achieved the levels of total output of the late fifties even by 1965. At the same time, of course, population has been increasing rapidly and this has meant deep stringency in the Chinese economy, particularly with her continuing emphasis on the importance of investment above consumption. Every indication, moreover, is that agricultural production still remains a major unsolved problem.

At present (1966), it seems fair to say that quite different assessments of the relative success or failure of India's and China's efforts are possible. Because of the disastrous harvest of 1965/66, there may be a tendency to underrate India's progress and to forget the important strides she has in fact been making over the past 15 years. Conversely, China's aggressive international stance, her testing of the atomic bomb and her recovery from the crisis of the great leap forward, make her seem a good deal more formidable economically than the whole record since 1952 justifies. The frenetic and fanatical quality of domestic life in China at the present time has an almost pathological quality; one has to wonder whether orderly economic development can proceed under such auspices.

In two respects, China probably does have advantages over India for the immediate future. One advantage is that her government is a highly powerful instrument that seems capable of exercising great influence and control over the mass of the society. One can guess that such a government could be enormously effective in, say, promoting a huge campaign for birth

16 See Ta-Chung Lin and Kung-Chia Yeh, *The Economy of the Chinese Mainland: National Income and Economic Development, 1933-1959* (Princeton: Princeton University Press, 1965), esp. pp. 119-124.

control should it choose to do so. By contrast, India's milder leadership and her more democratic political structure make the achievement of national objectives a somewhat more cumbersome task. The second advantage is that China, having no international support, has had to learn herself how to raise her rate of investment. She has been accomplishing a task that India is only now beginning to confront in a wholehearted way. This gives her an advantage in both time and experience, and perhaps also inures her to the hardships that development sometimes requires.

The other side of the coin is that always central problem of agriculture. Despite her current difficulties, India seems to have learned some important lessons in the management of her agricultural sector and progress may now be forthcoming. But what of China? So far, the history of mankind suggests that state control and collectivization face inherent difficulties in the agricultural sphere. The Soviet Union, as we know, has always been eminently more successful in coping with its industrial sector than with its farmers. Should the difficulty be inherent in the system, then the problem which the Chinese face would be infinitely more serious than it ever was in Russia because she is starting from a much lower level and she has, and will continue to have, many, many more hungry mouths to feed.

AN IMPORTANT MORAL

Whatever the final lesson of the Chinese experience proves to be, the record of both countries makes it quite clear that the process of "getting started" in a modern underdeveloped country is fraught with difficulties. China has plunged headlong into the task and incurred heavy and perhaps insupportable costs. India, more moderate and humanistic, has achieved only limited gains and even these would not have been possible had not a high fraction of her investment needs been met from abroad.

The moral of all this? Ultimately, of course, the moral implications of such matters as these must be reserved for each individual's judgment. Still, it is hard to avoid the conclusion that the assistance which the more developed countries of the world, and the United States in particular, have been giving to countries like India is an imperative at the present time and is likely to remain an imperative for decades to come. To be effective, moreover, aid must be looked at not as just a temporary stop-gap but as a long-run commitment. Even *with* such aid, many of these countries face a long battle against difficult odds; *without* it, they would have reason to despair. This is not to say that desperate men do not have alternatives. After all, China has weathered a major crisis without assistance from abroad. It is simply to say that it would be a deep human tragedy if, through a lack of vision or compassion in the advanced countries, the poor nations of the world were to decide that the insupportable costs of China's way would have to be supported after all.

Selected Reading

Deane, Phyllis, *The First Industrial Revolution.* (Cambridge: Cambridge University Press, 1965.) A survey account of the English Industrial Revolution, including some recent quantitative work in this field.

Fei, John, and G. Ranis, *Development of the Labor Surplus Economy.* (Homewood, Ill.: Irwin, 1964.) An elaborate, mainly theoretical, study of the "labor surplus" economy.

Government of India Planning Commission. This Commission publishes many documents including the Indian Five Year Plans, a reading of which will bring home to the student the concrete problems faced by the underdeveloped nations as they attempt to achieve economic growth.

Higgins, Benjamin, *Economic Development.* (New York: Norton, 1959.) An intermediate and comprehensive (800-page) textbook on economic development which includes a treatment of the major theories of economic growth and a long discussion of the many policy issues facing modern underdeveloped countries.

Hirschman, Albert O., *The Strategy of Economic Development.* (New Haven: Yale University Press, 1958.) The case for "unbalanced" growth is presented here as are many other stimulating insights into the problems of underdeveloped countries.

Kuznets, Simon, *Six Lectures on Economic Growth.* (Glencoe, Ill.: The Free Press, 1959.) One of the numerous books and articles by a distinguished scholar of growth trends in both advanced and underdeveloped countries; these lectures touch on such topics as the measurement of economic growth, the rapidity of growth in different countries, rates of capital formation, and changes in the quantitative importance of the different sectors of growing economies.

Lockwood, W. W., *The Economic Development of Japan: Growth and Structural Change, 1869-1938.* (Princeton: Princeton University Press, 1954.) A splendid historical analysis of the growth of the modern Japanese economy.

North, Douglass C., *Growth and Welfare in the American Past.* (Englewood Cliffs, N.J.: Prentice-Hall, 1966.) Subtitled, "A New Economic History," this book attempts to apply modern methods to the study of American growth.

Nurske, Ragnar, *Problems of Capital Formation in Underdeveloped Areas.* (New York: Oxford University Press, 1953.) A seminal work in the development field emphasizing such concepts as vicious circles of poverty, balanced growth, and disguised unemployment.

Pirenne, Henri, *Economic and Social History of Medieval Europe.* (New York: Harcourt, Brace, 1956.) A brilliant summary account of economic changes in Europe in the Middle Ages with special attention to the growth of commerce and urban life.

Abramowitz, Moses, "Resource and Output Trends in the United States since 1870," 20n

Africa: comparison with Latin America, 90; contrasts in living, 86, 86n; per-capita output, 82, (table) 83; population, 80, 86-88

Agriculture: balance with industry, 95-97, 99; relationship to development and industry, 22, 26; and the Soviet Union, 55, 56, 115; state-controlled, 55, 56, 94, 115; U.S. percentages, 63, 64

Aid (see also Foreign aid): to China, 115; to India, (table) 105, 115; international, 88, 89; U.S. loans and grants, 88

Annual real investment, defined, 11

Arkwright, Richard, 18, 48

Ashton, T. S., The Industrial Revolution, 48, 48n

Asia: comparison with Latin America, (table) 90; economic progress, 2; per capita output, 1957, (table) 83, 84, 98; population, 87, 88; population policy, 97

Birth rate: Malthus' and Ricardo's theories, 25-27; reasons for decline, 62n; reduction in Japan, 98; and relation to economic development, 7n; U.S., 61, 62, 69, 78

Bohm-Bawerk, theories on production methods, 13n

Brazil (see Latin America)

Business cycles (see also Depressions), 35

Campbell, Robert W., Soviet Economic Power, 56, 56n

Capital: accumulation and ownership, 13n; British investments, 53; of India, 104-106; investment in underdeveloped countries, 88, 89, 99; methods of mobilization, 92, 93, 94, 99; production, 12, 13; rate of formation, 92ff; relation to technology, 12; role in output, 12; "roundabout processes," 12, 13; and State, 54; tangible goods, defined, 10

Capital accumulation, 28, 29; of Ancient Egypt, 31; consumption vs. investment, 14; costs, 14; defined, 11; development of society, 31, 32; foreign investments, U.S., 70; future of, 76-79; per worker, 78, 79; rate, uses of, 13; Soviet Union, 13; in underdeveloped countries, 29; U.S. private enterprise, 69, 70

Capital formation, inflation as mechanism, 93, 94, 99

Capital goods, as force of development, 4

Capital investment, intangible and tangible, 11, 92, 92n

Capitalism: misnomer for Western kind of economics, 13n; Russian transition to communism, 24; study of, 48

Carey, Henry Charles, 69

China (see also Asia, Communism): agriculture, 103, 104, 107, (table) 109, 109n, 110, 112-115; area, 102; authoritarianism, 101, 106, 107; birth control, 112; collectivi-

zation, 102-104; communes, 104, 110, 112; consumer goods, 110-115; consumption levels, 114, 114n, 115; contrast with India, 104; cost of development, 114, 115; crop failures, 114; economic backwardness, 103, 103n; economy, post-World War II, 101ff; First Five-Year Plan, (table) 109; foreign aid, 109, 115; goals, overtaking Great Britain, 102; industry, 103, 103n, 106, 107, 109, 110, 115; investment rate, 106, 106n, 107, 109; level of total output, 114; Marriage Law, 1950, 104; national income, 114, 114n, 115; per capita output, 113; population, 101, 110-113; private enterprise, 103, 103n; propaganda, 104; reported failures, 114, 115; reserves, foreign exchange, 109; and Russian aid, 106, 106n, 107; self-sufficiency, 106, 106n, 107; standard of living, 101; "statistical blackout," 104; Treaty of Nanking, 1842, 101; urbanization, 114

Choh-Ming Li, "China," Economic Development, 109, 109n

Church and state: and the Middle Ages, 41; "Protestant ethic," 42

Clark, Colin, Conditions of Economic Progress, 24, 24n, (table) 64

Class struggle (see Communism; Marx, Karl)

"Classical" theory of economics, 25-27

Collectivization, China, 103, 104
Colonialism, 88
Common Market, 71
Communism (see also China, Soviet Union): capital essential, 13n; Marx's theory, 24
Condliffe, John B., "New Zealand," 12n
Conservation, U.S., 9
Consumer, in developing economy, 33
Consumption, future, 75, 76; U.S., 70, 70n, 71
Cotton textile industry, England, 46, 46n; Great Britain imports (table) 50
Crompton, Samuel, 46n
Cultivation of world's lands, (table) 8

Death rate: Asia decline, 7; Malthus and Ricardo, 25-27; raising, 98n
Denison, Edward F., Sources of Economic Growth in the United States, (table) 75
Depression, U.S., 60
"Diminishing returns," law, 26, (fig.) 26n, 27
DuBridge, Lee, A., "Educational and Social Consequences), 73n
Duesenberry, James S., Income Saving and the Theory of Consumer Behavior, 85, 85n

Eckstein, Alexander, The National Income of Communist China, 101, 101n
Economic development: Asia, Europe, U.S., and Latin America compared, 3, 4; conditions of, 51; defined, 35; effect on population growth, 6; historical approach, 35, 40, 41; limitations of theories, 23; objectives, 91, 92; patterns of, 22; theories of Colin Clark, 24; and undeveloped countries, 37
Economic growth: advanced countries development, 40, 41; balanced growth theories, 94, 95, 96, 96n, 98; chronic nature of, 34; concentration on specific areas, 95, 96, 96n; future, (table) 75, 76-78; as historical abnormality, 26; instability, 33; long-run measurements, 50-51; modern theories of, 27, 38; paradox of poverty and growth, 34; process of expansion, 4, 22; self-promoting process, 32; tensions, 94, 95, 96, 96n

Economy (see Capital, Economic development, Economic growth, Industry)
Education: in developing economy, 32; relation to scientific progress, 18; research expenditures, 73, 74
Employment: distribution, U.S., (table) 64; in 19th century England, 48
Employment creation, 97
England: agriculture, 43, 44; economic pressures, 18th century, 46; factory system, 47; history of, 41ff; Industrial Revolution, 48, 49; industry, 44ff; raw cotton imports, (table) 50; Royal Academy 1660, 43; science, 44
Entrepreneur: defined, 19, 47; obsolescence of, 74n
Erie canal, 70
Erosion, in Latin America, 9
Expenditures, ceremonial, 31n
"External economies," defined, 33, 33n, 34

Fabricant, Solomon, "Basic Facts on Productivity Change," 20n
Ford, Henry, 19
Foreign aid (see Aid)

Galbraith, John Kenneth, Economic Development in Perspective, 91, 91n
Genmill, Robert F., "Prebisch on Commercial Policy for Less-Developed Countries," 95, 96, 96n
Germany, production, 52
Gerschenkron, Alexander, "Economic Backwardness in Historical Perspective," 57, 57n
Gilboy, Elizabeth W., and Edgar M. Hoover, "Population and Immigration," (fig.) 62
GNP (Gross National Product), U.S., 65, 66, 66n, (fig.) 67, 90
Goldsmith, Raymond, "The Growth of Reproducible Wealth in the U.S.A., from 1805 to 1950," 70, 70n
Government, framework for economic change, 36
Government of India Planning Commission, 102, 103, 103n
Growth process in U.S., elements, 75-78
Growth rate: future, 76, 77; GNP statistics, (table) 90; problems, 80-88

Haberler, Gottfried, International Trade and Economic Development, 85, 96, 96n
Hagen, Everett E., "Some Facts about Income Levels and Economic Growth," (table) 82, (table) 83
Hance, William A., African Economic Development, 31n
Hargreaves, James, 46n
Higgins, Benjamin, Economic Development, 90, 90n
Hirschman, Albert O., The Strategy of Economic Development, 95, 96, 96n
Hoffman, Walther G., British Industry 1700-1950, (fig.) 50, 51
Hollister, W. W., China's Gross National Product and Social Accounts, 1950-1957, 106, 106n
Hoover, Edgar M., and Elizabeth W. Gilboy, Population and Immigration, (fig.) 62
Hughes, Richard, "China Makes a 'Bitter Retreat,' " 112, 112n

Immigration: U.S., relation to population, 62, 62n
Income levels, U.S., averages, 66
India (see also Asia): area, 100, 101; "balance" of development, efforts, 107, 109; caste system, 101, 102, 104; Chinese border aggression, 105; defense expenditures, 113; democracy, 102; economy, post-World War II, 103ff, 111; employment, 11, 112; exports, 108, 109; "external assistance," (table) 105; Family Planning Program, 111, 111n; Five Year Plans, 102, 103, 105, 107-109; foreign aid, 113, 115; imports, 109; Industrial Policy Resolution, 103n; industry, 103, 103n; international investment sources, 104, 105; investment, comparison with China, 106; labor resources, 105; level of output, 113; objectives of, 103n; per capita output, 113; population, 113; problems, social and political, 102; rate of change, 102, 103; "sacred cow" problem, 101n; savings, domestic, 105; socialism, 102, 103, 103n; standard of living, post-World War II, 101; taxation, 105; unemployment, 111, 113

Indian Independence Acts, 101
Industrialization (*see also* Economic development, Technology, Capital, Economic growth, England, China, India, Soviet Union): private enterprise and state, 53
Industrial Revolution, 38; enclosures, 43, 44; in England, 18, 19; in Europe, 87; growth process of, 35-39; modern, 84*ff*; in Russia, 55; summary, 57, 58
Industry (*see also* England, Capital, Labor, Technology): balance with agriculture, 94-97, 99; factory system, 47, 48; handicraft, 97; organization, 15, 41; theories of Adam Smith, 15-17; in underdeveloped countries, 18, 30-32
Inflation, 32, 94, 99
Innovation (*see also* Inventions), 18-20: in developing economy, 33, 34
Interdependence, in sectors of economy, 96
Inventions: England, 44-46, 46*n*; practical needs, 46; U.S., 72, 73
Investment: contrast between *19*th and *20*th centuries, 88; future, 76, 77; India, international sources, 105, 106; and raising rate, 92*ff*

Japan: birth-rate reduction, 98; government and business, 52-54, 54*n*; growth rate, 52-64, 90; production, 52-54, 54*n*

Kay, John, 46*n*
Kendrick, John W., *Productivity Trends in the United States*, 73, 73*n*, 74
Klein, L. R., and R. F. Kosobud, "Some Econometrics of Growth: Great Ratios of Economics," 71, 71*n*
Korea, 101
Kuznets, Simon: "Long Term Changes in the National Product of the United States of America Since 1870," 70, 70*n*; theories on economic growth, 33, 36, 70, 70*n*

Labor: "classical" theory, 26; consumption and production, 14*n*; "diminishing returns" theory, 24; distribution, U.S., *1820-1950*, (*table*), 64; division of, 14; employment in *19*th century, 47; enclosures, 43; exploitation, 23; factory system, 47; improved conditions, 23; machinery as re-

placement, 23; mobilization of unemployed, 92; output per man-hour, 5, 74; over-abundance, 86, 87; per-capita productivity, 13; and population growth, 5; and underdeveloped countries, 86, 87; U.S., changes in occupation, (*table*) 63, 64, 64*n*; U.S., history, 60, 61
Laissez-faire system, 47-49
Land, U.S., acquisition, 69
Latin America: Brazil, land per capita, 81; comparison with Africa, 90; comparison with U.S., 91; Economic Commission for, 89, 90, 90*n*; economic growth, 90, 91; inflation, 93, 94; per-capita output, (*table*) 82, (*table*) 89-91; population, 81, 87-90; poverty, 82, 83
Leisure, problem, 65, 68, 78
Life expectancy (*see also* Birth rate, Death rate, Medicine, Public health), 7; underdeveloped countries, 81, 87-89; U.S., (*table*) 63, 78
Lockwood, W. W., *The Economic Development of Japan*, 52, 52*n*
Lopez, Robert S., "The Trade of Medieval Europe," 42*n*

Malenbaum, Wilfred, "India and China: Contrasts in Development," 106, 106*n*, 114, 115
Malthus, Thomas Robert: application of theories to India, Pakistan, 27, 38; *Essay on the Principle of Population*, 1798, 25; failure of theories, applied to U.S., 68
Mantoux, Paul, *Industrial Revolution in the Eighteenth Century*, (*table*) 50
Market and exchange mechanisms, 22
Market, national (*see also* Railroads): expanding, 31; U.S. *19*th century, 70, 78
Marriot, McKim, "Technological Change in Overdeveloped Rural Areas," 11*n*
Marx, Karl: and exploitation of labor, 24; faults of predictions, 24, 38; influence in China and Russia, 25
Medicine, relation to population growth, 7, 8
Minority groups, 29, 30
Mobility, U.S., 59, 60
Myrdal, Gunnar, *Economic Theory and Underdeveloped Regions*, 84, 84*n*, 85

Nationalization, danger to private investment, 88
Natural resources: Ceylon, Colombia, Indonesia, Peru, Jordan, Yemen, 81; changing nature of, 10; "classical" theory of economics, 25; "creation" of new uses, 10; cultivation of world's lands, (*table*) 8; discovery and utilization of, 9, 20; effect on development of land, 52; as force of development, 4; forests, 8, 9; minerals, 8, 9; and population growth, 6; soil, 8, 9; and Western civilization, 9
Newton, Isaac, 43
Nigeria, 87
Nurske, Ragnar, *Problems of Capital Formation in Underdeveloped Areas*, 85, 85*n*, 96, 96*n*, 97

Oil, French West Africa, Libya, Nigeria, 9, 10
Orwell, George, *1984*, 104

Pakistan, partition of India, 101
Patents (*see* Inventions)
Perry, Commodore Matthew C., 52
Peter the Great, 55
Politics: and power, 54; state intervention in Japan, 54*n*
Population: Asia, 87, 97-99; "classical" theory, 26; "disguised unemployment," 88, 88*n*; effect on economic development, 6, 8, 17; as factor in production, 4; of India and China, 100; per-capita output, *1957*, 82, (*table*) 83; relation to capital accumulation, 26; and underdeveloped countries, 87, 88, 92, 98, 99; U.S. growth, 60, 61, 62-69, 77, 78; U.S. *1800-1960*, (*fig.*) 62
Poverty, 27-29, 80, 81, 97, 98, 99; chronic nature of, 34; contrast between rich and poor countries, 81; paradox of growth and poverty, 34; removal of, 90; statistics, (*table*) 82, (*table*) 83, 84, 98, 99; *20*th century India and China, 103*ff*
Prebisch, Raoul, "The Role of Commercial Policies in Underdeveloped Countries," 95, 96, 96*n*
Production: and capital, 12; changes in use of, 14; in developed and undeveloped

countries, 11, 12; in England, 51; factors of, 10; in Germany, 52; in Japan, 52-54, 54*n*; labor, 4; long-run growth, 58; medieval systems of, 14, 15; new products, 74, 75; in Russia, 52; scale of, *defined*, 14*n*; specialization, *defined*, 14*n*; total industrial, England, *1760-1950*, (*fig.*) 50; U.S., 51, 61*ff*; U.S. GNP in constant prices (*fig.*) 66; U.S. output per capita in constant prices (*fig.*) 66; U.S. scale, 15, 59, 78

Productivity, factors affecting, 92*ff*

Profits (*see also* Marx, Karl), Marx's theories, 24, 25

Public health: progress, 87, 98; relation to population growth, 7

Railroads: in Europe, 52; expansion, 52, 53, 57; foreign investments, U.S., 70; national market, U.S., 71, 72; public funds, U.S., 70; unification, U.S., 71

Religion, and population problems, 97, 98

Research, 92*n*; in a developing economy, 33, 34

Ricardo, David: and application of theories to India and Pakistan, 27, 38; *Principles of Political Economy and Taxation*, 25, 26

Rostow, W. W.: and answers to Marx's theories, 25*n*; conditions necessary for economic change, 36; critical periods of various countries, (*table*) 37, 37*n*; *Stages of Economic Growth, The*, 25*n*; (*table*) 37

Russia (*see* Soviet Union)

Scale of production, *defined*, 14*n*

Schultz, Theodore W., "Economic Prospects of Primary Products," 96, 96*n*

Schumpeter, Joseph A., *Capitalism, Socialism and Democracy*, 74, 74*n*

Smith, Adam, *Wealth of Nations*, 15-17

Soviet Union: agriculture, 55, 56, 95, 115; aid to China, 106; capital accumulation, 13; changes in economic system, 54; competition with U.S., 56, 56*n*; concepts of economy, *defined*, 2, 55; entrepreneur, 19; heavy industry, 95; industrial problems, 115; rate of economic growth, 2, 55, 56, 56*n*; weaknesses, 56

Specialization, 14; *defined*, 14*n*; U.S. production, 15

Standards of living: Europe and North America, 6, 7; spread of Western techniques, 7; underdeveloped countries, 7

"Stationary" state of income (*see also* "Classical" theory), 27

Steel, production figures, 52

Synthetic materials, revolution in, 10

Ta-Chung Liu and Kung-Chia Yeh, "Preliminary Estimate of the National Income of the Chinese Mainland, 1952-1959," 114, 114*n*, 115

Taiwan, land per capita, 81

Tawney, R. H., *Religion and the Rise of Capitalism*, 42*n*

Taxation: future of, in U.S., 76, 77; and investment rate, 93, 99; in Russia, 55

Technology: acceleration in *18*th century England, 44, 45; adaptation in underdeveloped countries, 85*ff*, 98, 99; applied and pure science, 17, 18; change in developing economy, 32, 33, 39; difficulties in adaptation, 84*ff*, 99; education and research, 73, 74, 77, 89, 99; evolution, 52, 53, 73; factors, 4, 19; history of, 17; innovation and invention, 18; investment requirements, 91, 98, 99; rate of change, 19, 36; relation to capital, 12; relation to productivity, 74; revolutionary process, 19, 20; U.S. revolution, 71-73

Tensions in economy, arguments pro and con, 94, 95, 96, 96*n*, 97

"Terms of trade," *defined*, 96*n*

Totalitarianism: in China, 103, 103*n*; forcing of high growth rate, 93

Trade, expansion of, 42

Transport: Africa, 31; "extent of the market," 16; factors in development, 31

Underdeveloped countries (*see also* Africa, Asia, Latin America, China), 85*ff*; and "classical" theory of economics, 25-27

Underdevelopment, *defined*, 80, 81

Unemployment: causes, 24; in India, 105; and mobilization of labor, 92; relation to actual and potential output, 35; relation to population, 87; underdeveloped countries, 86; in U.S., 78

United States, 61*ff*

Urbanization, U.S., 63, (*table*) 63

USSR (*see* Soviet Union, Communism)

Weber, Max, *The Protestant Ethic and the Spirit of Capitalism*, 42*n*

Wedgwood, Josiah, 45